Praise for
The Happy Sandwich

"Jason is pure joy! He radiates happiness, especially when it comes to cooking. His recipes are easy, fun, and absolutely delicious."
—Robin Roberts, anchor of ABC's *Good Morning America*

"Authentic and scrumptious with a side of good vibes. The sandwich book everyone has been craving!"
—Chef Chris Valdes, *Food Network Star* finalist

"A knife and fork is not required to enjoy a gourmet meal, but you will need a napkin to wipe your smile clean after the first delicious bite! Jason's recipes are as bold, colorful, and full of personality as he is!"
—Lara Lyn Carter, creator of *Skinny Southern*

Published by Familius LLC, www.familius.com

PO Box 1249, Reedley, CA 93654

Familius books are available at special discounts for bulk purchases,
whether for sales promotions or for family or corporate use.
For more information, contact Familius Sales
at orders@familius.com.

Library of Congress Control Number: 2020952406

Print ISBN 9781641704601

Ebook ISBN 978-1-64170-508-0

KF 978-1-64170-528-8

FE 978-1-64170-548-6

Printed in China

Edited by Peg Sandkam and Spencer Skeen

Cover and book design by Mara Harris

10 9 8 7 6 5 4 3 2 1

First Edition

The Happy Sandwich

Happy

JASON GOLDSTEIN

This book is dedicated to my husband, Tom, who is my greatest support and recipe tester. You always believe in me and are the secret ingredient to all of my success. I am so grateful for you! Love you forever!

Also, love you, Charlie, my favorite sous-chef in the world!

Special thank you to:
Lisa Hammer, for making this journey possible.
You are a shining light in my life and career, and I appreciate you.

Nikki Incandela, for helping edit the photos!
You are the best and I am grateful for you!

Thank you to my mom, sister, brother-in-law,
Sydney, Tyler, and Mitchel for always cheering me on!

Table of *Contents*

CHAPTER 1: SLOW COOKER SANDWICHES

CHAPTER 2: SHEET PAN SANDWICHES

CHAPTER 3: GRLLED CHEESE SANDWICHES

CHAPTER 4: NO-COOK SANDWICHES

CHAPTER 5: NO BREAD SANDWICHES

CHAPTER 6: CONDIMENTS

Chapter 1: *Slow Cooker* Sandwiches

The slow cooker is your personal chef and life coach: Not only does it cook meals for you while you are busy at work but it also leaves you more time for self-care!

Eggplant *Parm* Sandwich

INGREDIENTS:

Fill It Up!

1 large eggplant

1 teaspoon pepper

3 tablespoons extra virgin olive oil

1 teaspoon salt

½ cup ricotta cheese

2 cloves of garlic

10 basil leaves

1 teaspoon oregano

1 handful parsley

½ teaspoon red pepper flakes

1 egg

2 cups bread crumbs

½ cup parmesan cheese, shredded

2 cups of your favorite tomato sauce

1 pound mozzarella cheese, cut into small cubes

Top It off!

10 slices sourdough bread

1 cup of your favorite tomato sauce

¼ cup parmesan cheese, shredded

4–5 basil leaves, chopped

This recipe is dedicated to Mama Goldstein, who let us have the cheesiest thing we could think of once a week. This taught us we did not have to wait till the weekend to have fun!

INSTRUCTIONS

1. Cut the eggplant into one-inch chunks.

2. Add the eggplant, pepper, olive oil, and salt to a pan on medium heat. Cook for about 3 minutes until the eggplant is browned and soft. Set aside to cool (approximately 10 minutes).

3. Put the eggplant, ricotta, garlic, basil, oregano, parsley, red pepper flakes, egg, bread crumbs, ½ cup of parmesan, and a pinch of salt into a food processor.

4. Pulse until mixed and a thick paste forms with small chunks of eggplant. *NOTE: The mixture will be thick but still wet.*

5. Line the slow cooker with tin foil and add the eggplant mixture. Shape the mixture into a loaf using the tin foil.

6. Pour 2 cups of the tomato sauce on top of the loaf.

7. Add the mozzarella on top of the sauce, cover, and cook on low for 8 hours.

8. Once cooking is complete, top with more parmesan and chopped basil.

9. Slice the eggplant loaf into thick slices and place a slice on a piece of bread. Top with some tomato sauce and more parmesan cheese. Finish off with another slice of bread and the sandwich is ready to enjoy!

LEFTOVERS: Freeze for up to 6 months stored in a Ziploc bag! To enjoy, thaw overnight in the refrigerator or place frozen in the slow cooker with ¼ cup of chicken broth and cook on low for 6 hours.

Tip!

SKIP THE SEAR! Making ribs in the slow cooker makes life so much easier and skips so many steps of the traditional method! To get the perfect, saucy cooked ribs, lean them around the sides of the slow cooker so they sear and can steam from the liquid on the bottom. This way you can take them out of the slow cooker and skip searing them.

BBQ *Rib* Sandwich
with Homemade Garlic Bread

INGREDIENTS:

Slow Cooker BBQ Pork Ribs

Fill It Up!

1 teaspoon salt

1 teaspoon pepper

1 teaspoon garlic powder

1 rack St. Louis cut ribs

No-Cook BBQ Sauce, divided
(see page 123 in the
condiments section)

Top It Off!

Old School 15-Minute Garlic
Bread Bun (see below for
recipe)

15 pickle slices

*Old School 15-Minute
Garlic Bread Bun*

1 stick unsalted butter, melted

1 teaspoon dried oregano

1 teaspoon garlic powder

½ teaspoon red pepper flakes

1 teaspoon salt

1 teaspoon pepper

1 baguette

1 handful fresh parsley, chopped

INSTRUCTIONS

Slow Cooker BBQ Pork Ribs

1. Sprinkle the salt, pepper, and garlic powder all over both sides of the ribs.

2. Smother both sides of the ribs with half a cup of the BBQ sauce.

3. Place the ribs in the slow cooker leaning against the sides. Then pour the remaining BBQ sauce on top of the ribs.

4. Cook for 6 hours on low.

5. Once cooked, pull out the bones while trying to keep the meat in one piece.

6. Place the meat on one half of the garlic bread, top with pickles, and place the other half of the loaf on top.

7. Cut the loaf into four portions and enjoy!

Old School 15-Minute Garlic Bread Bun

1. Preheat the oven to 350 degrees.

2. Combine the butter, oregano, garlic powder, red pepper flakes, salt, and pepper in a small bowl.

3. Slice the bread in half lengthwise and brush the butter over both sides of the bread, including the crusts.

4. Place the bread on a baking sheet and bake on the top rack of the oven for 15 minutes. *NOTE: Make sure you watch the bread so it does not burn!*

5. Once the bread is cooked, sprinkle with parsley.

LEFTOVERS: Freeze for up to 6 months stored in a Ziploc bag! Thaw overnight in the refrigerator or place frozen in a slow cooker with ¼ cup of chicken broth and cook on low for 6 hours.

"Laughter is brightest
where food is best.
—Irish Proverb

INGREDIENTS:

Fill It Up!

1 can (13.5 ounces) coconut milk

Juice of 1 lime

4 tablespoons Thai Kitchen red curry paste, divided

2 pounds ground beef

1 handful mint, chopped

1 handful cilantro, chopped

2 cloves of garlic, finely chopped

1 inch of ginger, finely chopped

1 egg

2 cups bread crumbs

4 scallions, chopped

1 teaspoon salt

1 teaspoon pepper

Top It Off!

Mayonnaise

4 sub rolls

1 cucumber, chopped

1 handful shredded carrots

Thai *Curry* Meatball Sub

INSTRUCTIONS

1. Combine the coconut milk, lime juice, and 2 tablespoons of the red curry paste in the slow cooker.

2. In a large bowl, mix the remaining red curry paste, ground beef, mint, cilantro, garlic, ginger, egg, bread crumbs, scallions, salt, and pepper.

3. Roll the ground beef mixture into golf ball-size meatballs and place them in the slow cooker. Spoon the prepared sauce over all the meatballs.

4. Cover and cook on low for 7 hours.

5. When done cooking, slather mayonnaise on both sides of each sub roll, add meatballs, and drizzle on some of the sauce; sprinkle some cucumber and carrots on top and enjoy!

LEFTOVERS: The slow cooker is the perfect vessel for this recipe; it makes enough for dinner today and leftovers on a busy day. When I make these meatballs, I eat half now and freeze the rest in a Ziploc bag. Just take the frozen meatballs out the night before or put the frozen meatballs in the slow cooker for 6 hours on low and come home to find meatball magic!

Tip!

PURCHASE PORK STEW MEAT! Pork stew meat is the same as a big chunk of pork shoulder! The only difference is the butcher has already cut it up into chunks. The smaller the chunks of pork, the more seasoned they will be.

INGREDIENTS:

Fill It Up!

2 sweet potatoes

3 pounds pork stew meat

2 teaspoons salt

2 teaspoons pepper

3 cups tomatillo sauce

3 scallions, chopped

1 handful cilantro, chopped

Juice of 1 lime

Top It Off!

5 sub rolls

5 slices cheddar cheese

LEFTOVERS: You can use half of the pork for the sandwiches and the other half over rice for a pork burrito bowl later in the week! You can freeze leftovers for up to 6 months in a Ziploc bag. Thaw overnight in the refrigerator or place frozen in a slow cooker with ¼ cup of chicken broth and cook on low for 6 hours.

Salsa Verde *Pork & Sweet Potato* Sandwich

INSTRUCTIONS

1. Cut the sweet potatoes into chunks and combine them with the pork stew meat, salt, pepper, and tomatillo sauce in the slow cooker.

2. Place the lid on the slow cooker and cook on low for 6 hours.

3. Once cooked, add the scallions, cilantro, and lime juice. You can then either shred the pork or leave it whole.

4. Spoon some sauce from the bottom of the slow cooker onto both sides of each roll, then add some pork and sweet potatoes, followed by a slice of cheddar cheese.

LOAD THE SLOW COOKER THE NIGHT BEFORE! There are two amazing reasons to do this. First, you can just take it out of the refrigerator and turn it on so you have more "you time" in the morning. The less to do in the morning, the less you need to rush. Second, all the flavors get to marinate overnight and you get a much yummier recipe. If you season right before you cook, only the outside of the meat will have flavor. But if you season overnight, the flavors will permeate throughout the meat.

Tip!

MEAT SEASONING HACK!
Here is a great chef secret to seasoning your beef all the way through! For short ribs, steak, or even chicken, salt the meat heavily the night before and place in the refrigerator uncovered. This will give the salt time to penetrate through the meat and will give you much more flavorful results!

INGREDIENTS:

Fill It Up!

4 teaspoons salt, divided

4 teaspoons pepper, divided

3 pounds beef short ribs

1 can (28 ounces) whole
    tomatoes

1 teaspoon garlic powder

1 teaspoon honey

1 teaspoon oregano

½ teaspoon red pepper flakes

10 fresh basil leaves,
    torn by hand

1 large white onion, chopped

2 carrots, chopped

1 handful parsley, chopped

Top It Off!

Mayonnaise

10 slices sourdough bread,
    toasted

10 slices provolone cheese

1 handful arugula

10–15 pickle slices

Short Rib Sandwich

INSTRUCTIONS

1. Preheat the oven to 400 degrees.

2. Combine 3 teaspoons of salt and 3 teaspoons of pepper in a small bowl. Rub the seasonings on both sides of the short ribs.

3. Place the ribs on a sheet tray on the middle rack of the oven and bake for 15 minutes or until brown; this will sear the meat without messing with oil on the stovetop.

4. Place the tomatoes, garlic powder, honey, oregano, red pepper flakes, basil, onions, carrots, and 1 teaspoon each of salt and pepper into the slow cooker. Mix together while breaking up the tomatoes with a spoon or potato masher.

5. Nestle the short ribs into the sauce.

6. Cover and cook for 8 hours on low.

7. Once the ribs are cooked, remove from the slow cooker, top with parsley, and shred.

8. Spread mayonnaise on two slices of toasted sourdough bread. Top one bread slice with two slices of provolone cheese and some arugula, pickles, and shredded short ribs. Pour some juice over the short ribs and top with the remaining prepared bread slice.

LEFTOVERS: This can be frozen for up to 3 months stored in a Ziploc bag! Thaw overnight in the refrigerator.

Chicken *Parm* Sub

INGREDIENTS:

Fill It Up!

½ cup ricotta cheese

4 tablespoons parmesan cheese, shredded

2 eggs

1 teaspoon red pepper flakes

3 cloves of garlic, finely chopped

1 tablespoon oregano

1 handful parsley, chopped

10 basil leaves, chopped

Salt

Black pepper

2 pounds ground chicken

½ cup panko bread crumbs

2 jars of your favorite marinara sauce, divided

Top It Off!

4 sub rolls

1 pound mozzarella cheese, shredded

INSTRUCTIONS

1. In a large bowl, mix together the ricotta, parmesan, eggs, red pepper flakes, garlic, oregano, parsley, basil, and a pinch each of salt and pepper.

2. Add the chicken, panko, and a heavy pinch each of salt and pepper. Gently combine all the ingredients until mixed well.

3. Roll the mixture into golf ball-size meatballs and set aside.

4. Pour one jar of marinara sauce into the slow cooker. Nestle as many meatballs as you can next to each other in the sauce.

5. Pour half of the second jar of sauce over the meatballs.

6. Layer the remaining meatballs on the sauce and then top the meatballs with the remaining sauce.

7. Cover the slow cooker and cook on low for 4 hours.

8. Once the meatballs are cooked, preheat the oven to 500 degrees.

9. Layer meatballs on each sub roll. Top with the cooked sauce, mozzarella cheese, and the top of the roll. Toast in the oven until cheese is bubbly.

LEFTOVERS: Freeze for up to 6 months in a Ziploc bag! Thaw overnight in the refrigerator or cook in the slow cooker with extra marinara sauce for 6 hours on low.

JUICY MEATBALLS EVERY TIME! Adding ricotta cheese to the meatball mixture will ensure juicy, fabulous meatballs. The ricotta cheese melts in and saves the traditional step of soaking the bread crumbs in milk.

"There is no sincerer love
than the love of food."
—George Bernard Shaw

INGREDIENTS:

Fill It Up!

2 tablespoons oregano

2 teaspoons salt

2 teaspoons pepper

2 pounds first cut brisket

2 large spanish onions, chopped, divided

2 large carrots, chopped, divided

2 packets onion soup mix

1 pint mushrooms, sliced

Top It Off!

Mayonnaise

5 sub rolls

10 slices pepper jack cheese

1 handful parsley, chopped

LEFTOVERS: Cut up extra meat and fry it in a pan with some eggs for a twist on a steak and eggs breakfast the next day! The meat can be frozen for up to 6 months stored in a Ziploc bag. Thaw overnight in the refrigerator or place frozen in a slow cooker with ¼ cup of chicken broth and cook on low for 6 hours.

French Dip Brisket Sandwich

This is a version of Mama Goldstein's recipe from my childhood. She would cook the brisket for hours covered in tin foil and baste every hour. I took this recipe and made it easier to make on a busy day. With a slow cooker, just set it and forget it!

INSTRUCTIONS

1. Mix together the oregano, salt, and pepper; pat over both sides of the brisket.

2. Add half of the onions, half of the carrots, one packet of the onion soup mix, a pinch of salt, and a pinch of pepper to the bottom of the slow cooker. Mix to combine.

3. Rub the second packet of onion soup mix onto both sides of the brisket and place the brisket into the slow cooker.

4. Top the brisket with the remaining onions and carrots, the mushrooms, and a pinch each of salt and pepper.

5. Cover and cook for 6 hours on low.

6. Once it is done, cover with tin foil and let rest for 20 minutes, so the juices stay in the meat. Then cut against the grain (opposite the direction the meat strands are going).

7. Pour the broth from the slow cooker into small bowls for dipping.

8. Spread mayonnaise on the inside of each roll, add 2 slices of pepper jack cheese, sprinkle on some parsley, and top it off with slices of brisket.

9. Dip the sandwich in the broth and enjoy!

INGREDIENTS:

Fill It Up!

2 pounds ground chicken

3 scallions, chopped

1 large red onion, chopped

3 cloves of garlic, chopped

1 tablespoon grated ginger

2 tablespoons tomato paste

1 can (14.5 ounces) diced tomatoes

1 teaspoon salt

1 teaspoon pepper

4 tablespoons harissa paste, divided

1 cup + 2 handfuls spinach, divided

3 tablespoons honey

½ cup feta cheese, crumbled

Top It Off!

Mayonnaise

4 hamburger buns, toasted

1 handful spinach

Feta cheese, crumbled

Honey Harissa Sloppy Joe

INSTRUCTIONS

1. Place the chicken, scallions, onions, garlic, ginger, tomato paste, tomatoes, salt, pepper, 2 tablespoons of harissa paste, and 1 cup of spinach in the slow cooker. Mix well until combined.

2. Cover and cook on low for 6 hours.

3. Once cooked, add the honey, feta, 2 tablespoons of harissa paste, and 2 handfuls of spinach to the slow cooker; mix everything together.

4. Slather mayonnaise on both the top and bottom of each bun.

5. Place a pinch of spinach on the bottom of each bun, add a large scoop of sloppy joe, and top with feta. Close the sandwich and enjoy!

LEFTOVERS: Freeze for up to 6 months in a Ziploc bag! Thaw overnight in the refrigerator or place frozen in the slow cooker with ¼ cup of chicken broth and cook for 6 hours on low.

CHICKEN HACK! Use ground chicken with a higher percentage of fat. This usually means it is a combination of both white and dark meat, which will help make it juicier.

Open Face French Onion Soup

This recipe is dedicated to my dad. My mom tells me stories about how much he loved french onion soup. When he finally traveled to France, she told me he ordered it for breakfast, lunch, and dinner!

INGREDIENTS:

Fill It Up!

3 pounds vidalia onions, sliced

1 tablespoon thyme, chopped

2 cloves of garlic, crushed

2 tablespoons brown sugar

2 tablespoons butter

1 teaspoon balsamic vinegar

1 teaspoon salt

1 teaspoon pepper

Top It Off!

4 tablespoons dijon mustard

4 slices sourdough bread

3 scallions, chopped

2 cups gruyère cheese, grated

2 teaspoons thyme, chopped

INSTRUCTIONS

1. Mix the onions, thyme, garlic, brown sugar, butter, balsamic vinegar, salt, and pepper in the slow cooker.

2. Cover and cook on low for 10 hours.

3. Once the onions are cooked, preheat the oven to 500 degrees.

4. Smear some dijon mustard on each slice of sourdough bread and place the bread on a sheet tray.

5. Place a heaping mound of the onion mixture onto each slice of bread.

6. Top with scallions, lots of cheese, and some thyme.

7. Place on the top rack of the oven for a minute or two until the cheese melts. Enjoy!

LEFTOVERS: Freeze the onions for up to 6 months in a Ziploc bag! Thaw overnight in the refrigerator or cook from frozen in a slow cooker with ¼ cup of chicken broth on low for 6 hours.

Slow Cooker Spicy Apricot Ham

INGREDIENTS:

Fill It Up!

½ cup apricot or orange jam

3 tablespoons spicy honey
(or 3 tablespoons honey and
1 teaspoon sriracha)

1 5- to 7-pound spiral ham

Top It Off!

Mayonnaise

16 slices white bread

16 slices swiss cheese

This recipe illustrates my mantra in life: *Simplicity in the kitchen and simplicity in life*. Literally just three ingredients go in the slow cooker and that is it! When we go through our day, sometimes we over-complicate things. When this happens, try to simplify things in your life and you will really see what you are grateful for!

INSTRUCTIONS

1. Combine the jam and honey in a small bowl.

2. Spread the jam and honey mixture all over the ham.

3. Place the ham in the slow cooker and cook on low for 6 hours and 30 minutes.

4. When done, baste with the sauce.

5. Spread mayonnaise on the top and bottom slices of the bread.

6. Place a slice of swiss cheese on the bottom slice of bread and layer lots of ham on top.

7. Add another slice of cheese and top with the remaining prepared slice of bread.

LEFTOVERS: This is a perfect meal for a hectic weeknight dinner! Lots of leftovers make great hash, pasta, or lunchtime sandwiches. The ham can be frozen up to 6 months in a Ziploc bag. Thaw overnight in the refrigerator or cook from frozen in the slow cooker with ¼ cup of chicken broth on low for 6 hours.

RECIPE HACK! Use precooked spiral ham so you don't have to worry about the ham cooking all the way through.

Chapter 2: *Sheet Pan* Sandwiches

Cooking everything on a sheet pan makes for less clean up and more time with your family! Here's a fun idea for your next date night: grab a couple of forks and eat right out of the sheet pan while you watch TV!

Mexican Chicken Sausage & Peppers Sub

INGREDIENTS:

Fill It Up!

1 red pepper, cut in strips

1 orange pepper, cut in strips

1 jalapeño, deseeded and cut in strips

1 large white onion, sliced

1 teaspoon garlic powder

2 teaspoons adobo sauce with chipotles

1 teaspoon salt

1 teaspoon pepper

3 tablespoons extra virgin olive oil

8 smoked chicken sausage links

Juice of 1 lime

1 handful cilantro, chopped

Top It Off!

Arugula Pesto (see page 124 in the condiments section)

4 sub rolls, sliced horizontally

INSTRUCTIONS

1. Preheat the oven to 400 degrees.

2. Mix the red and orange peppers, jalapeños, onions, garlic powder, adobo sauce, salt, pepper, and olive oil on the sheet pan.

3. Mix the sausage links with the veggies so they get coated with the seasonings, then nestle on top of the veggies.

4. Bake for 20 minutes, turning the sausage halfway through.

5. When done baking, squeeze fresh lime juice and sprinkle cilantro over the sausage.

6. Slather some pesto over the bread, stuff with sausage, and enjoy!

RECIPE TIP! Using precooked sausage saves 20–30 minutes of cooking time and gives you more time to dream big! Also, because the inside is cooked already, it gives the outside a more caramelized, crispy skin.

Crispy Oven-Fried Shrimp

INGREDIENTS:

Fill It Up!

1 pound large shrimp, peeled

1 cup flour

2 eggs

1 cup crushed Ritz crackers

6 teaspoons salt, divided

6 teaspoons pepper, divided

3 teaspoons oregano, divided

3 teaspoons garlic powder, divided

Juice of half a lemon

Top It Off!

4 sub rolls

Mama Goldstein's Russian Dressing (see page 121 in the condiments section)

½ cup shredded lettuce

INSTRUCTIONS

1. Preheat the oven to 400 degrees and spray a sheet tray with cooking spray.

2. Season the shrimp with salt and pepper.

3. Put the flour, eggs, and crushed crackers onto separate plates. To each plate, add 2 teaspoons of salt, 2 teaspoons of pepper, 1 teaspoon of oregano, and 1 teaspoon of garlic powder.

4. Dip and coat each shrimp in the flour, then egg, then crackers.

5. Place the shrimp on the sheet tray without touching; spray the shrimp with cooking spray.

6. Bake for 5–6 minutes, then flip and spray again with cooking spray. Bake for an additional 5–6 minutes.

7. Sprinkle with a little salt and a little lemon juice.

8. Slather the rolls with Russian dressing, stack the shrimp on the roll, and top with lettuce.

BECOME A SEASONING MASTER! Finding ways to quickly add seasoning and flavor with less work is always key. I use Ritz crackers because they are already flavored with buttery, salty fabulousness. The more flavor, the better you feel about your success in the kitchen!

Tip!

RECIPE TIP! To get a dry-aged flavor at home, heavily season the steak with salt the night before. Leave the steak uncovered on a plate in the refrigerator overnight; this allows the salt to permeate throughout the beef and draw out water. Leaving it uncovered allows air to circulate around the steak and helps the salt sink in.

NYC *Cheesesteak*

INGREDIENTS:

Fill It Up!

4 scallions, roughly chopped

1 large red onion, sliced

1 teaspoon garlic powder

5 tablespoons extra virgin olive oil, divided

2 teaspoons salt, divided

2 teaspoons pepper, divided

1 tablespoon of your favorite grill seasoning

1 16-ounce NY strip steak, about an inch thick

Top It Off!

2 sub rolls, cut in half

Extra Creamy Homemade Mayonnaise (see page 126 in the condiments section)

1 cup arugula

¼ pound blue cheese, cut into large chunks

This recipe is dedicated to my husband, Tom! His first New York steakhouse experience was with my mom and me on his birthday. I will never forget the look on his face as he ate a huge juicy and buttery steak. It was culinary nirvana!

INSTRUCTIONS

1. Preheat the oven to 500 degrees.

2. Add the scallions, onions, garlic powder, 3 tablespoons of olive oil, 1 teaspoon of salt, and 1 teaspoon of pepper to the sheet pan. Mix the ingredients together and spread over one half of the sheet pan.

3. In a small bowl, mix together the grill seasoning, 2 tablespoons of olive oil, 1 teaspoon of salt, and 1 teaspoon of pepper; sprinkle onto both sides of the steak. Place the steak on the other half of the sheet pan.

4. Put the sheet tray on the top rack of the oven for 4 minutes, then flip the steak and cook for 4 more minutes for medium rare (for medium, cook 5–6 minutes per side). Take the steak out of the oven and let it rest for 10 minutes (to keep the juices inside) before cutting into it.

5. To assemble the sandwich, slather both sides of the bread with mayonnaise. Add some arugula to the bottom roll, followed by some steak and onions, and finally some of the blue cheese. Add the top half of the roll and enjoy!

Taco *Chicken* Salad

INGREDIENTS:

Fill It Up!

3 tablespoons olive oil

2 teaspoons salt

2 teaspoons pepper

4 teaspoons chili blend seasoning or taco seasoning, divided

4 large chicken breasts

2 cups store-bought pico de gallo

3 scallions, chopped

Juice of 1 lime

3 tablespoons Extra Creamy Homemade Mayonnaise (see page 126 in the condiments section)

Top It Off!

4 croissants, sliced

Extra Creamy Homemade Mayonnaise

4 slices tomato

4 slices pepper jack cheese

INSTRUCTIONS

1. Preheat the oven to 375 degrees.

2. In a small bowl, combine the oil, salt, pepper, and 3 teaspoons of chili seasoning.

3. Coat the chicken in the mixture; place on a sheet pan and cook for 35 minutes. *NOTE: Spread the chicken apart so it roasts rather than steams.*

4. Cool and then shred the chicken.

5. In a bowl, combine the pico de gallo, scallions, lime juice, mayonnaise, 1 teaspoon of chili seasoning, and a pinch each of salt and pepper.

6. Mix the chicken in the dressing.

7. Place some chicken on a croissant smeared with extra mayonnaise; top with tomato and a slice of pepper jack cheese.

COOKING TIP! Salsa, tomatillo sauce, marinara sauce, and taco seasoning are all totally fine from a jar. This makes life so much easier and makes for less time in the kitchen!

Sheet Pan Bacon-Infused Burger

INGREDIENTS:

1 package frozen french fries

Fill It Up!

5 strips bacon, raw

2 pounds ground beef

1 teaspoon salt

1 teaspoon pepper

Top It Off!

Burger Sauce (see page 123 in the condiments section)

4 slices cheddar cheese

Lettuce

Sliced red onion

Sliced tomato

4 burger buns

I call these my "dream big" burgers. I prepared the grilled version of this burger on *Good Morning America* with Robin Roberts. It was such an amazing experience, and it taught me that anything is possible. Dream big, because your dreams can become reality!

INSTRUCTIONS

1. Preheat the oven and cook the fries according to package instructions. Sprinkle the fries with salt and wrap in tin foil to keep them warm while you make the burgers; set to the side.

2. If needed, change the oven temperature to 400 degrees.

3. Add the bacon to a food processor or blender and pulse until a paste is formed.

4. In a large bowl, mix the bacon, beef, salt, and pepper. Form into four patties.

5. Add the patties to a sheet pan and drizzle with olive oil.

6. Cook for 10 minutes and then flip; cook another 5 minutes for medium rare or 7 minutes for medium.

7. Add the burger and some burger sauce, cheese, lettuce, onion, and tomato to each bun. Serve with fries and ketchup.

First we eat, then we do everything else.
—M. F. K. Fisher

INGREDIENTS:

Fill It Up!

22 small pepperoni slices, divided

12 eggs

½ cup heavy cream

1 cup shredded mozzarella

¼ teaspoon red pepper flakes

1 tablespoon garlic powder

1 tablespoon dried oregano

10 basil leaves, chopped

Salt

Pepper

½ cup parmesan cheese, grated

1 pint cherry or grape tomatoes, cut in half

Top It Off!

Homemade Pantry Ketchup (see page 120 in the condiments section)

4 round brioche rolls

4 slices provolone cheese

Sheet Pan Egg Pizza Sandwich

This is dedicated to my love of New York City. We live in Chelsea, NYC, and every day I walk down the streets saying, "I love NYC!" When creating this recipe, I thought of the aroma that comes from an authentic NYC pizza place. The extra seasonings you sprinkle on your slice of pizza—garlic powder, oregano, and red pepper seasoning—are in this recipe. Cheers to NYC pizza in sandwich form!

INSTRUCTIONS

1. Preheat the oven to 350 degrees and spray a large sheet pan with cooking spray.

2. Chop 12 pepperoni slices into smaller slices.

3. In a bowl, mix the sliced pepperoni, eggs, cream, mozzarella, red pepper flakes, garlic powder, oregano, a large pinch of salt, a large pinch of pepper, and 5 heaping tablespoons of parmesan.

4. Pour the egg mixture onto the prepared sheet pan. Top the mixture with the tomatoes, remaining pepperoni, and a little more parmesan cheese. Cook for 20 minutes or until the eggs are done.

5. Cut the eggs into squares a little larger than the size of your bun.

6. Put ketchup on both the top and bottom of each roll. Top with a couple egg squares and a slice of provolone; enjoy!

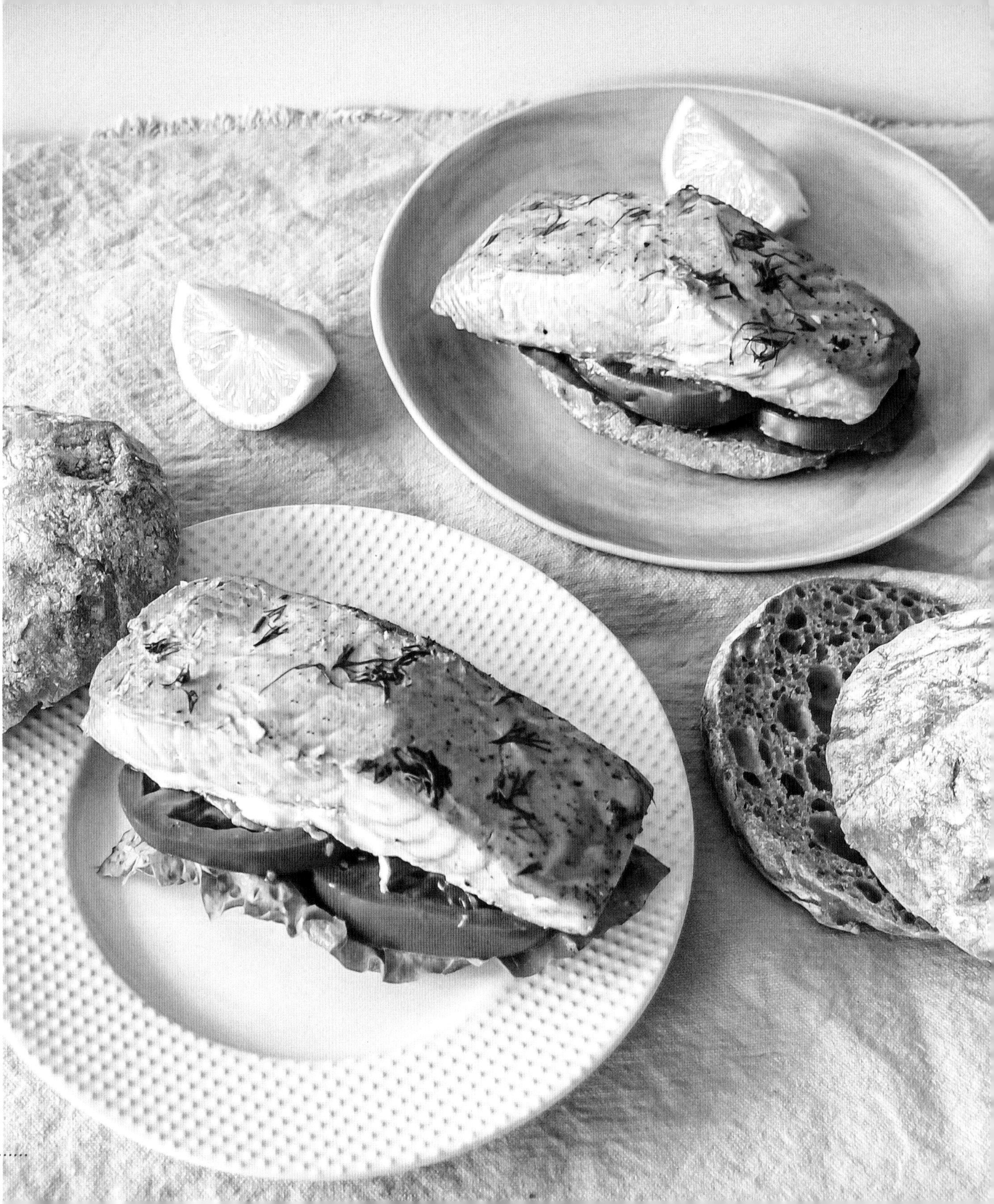

Dijon *Salmon* Sandwich

INGREDIENTS:

Fill It Up!

4 salmon fillets

Juice of half a lemon

2 tablespoons extra virgin olive oil

1 teaspoon salt

1 teaspoon pepper

Handful fresh dill, chopped, divided

4 tablespoons Dijon Honey Mustard (see page 124 in the condiments section)

Top It Off!

Dijon Honey Mustard

4 ciabatta rolls

Lettuce

Sliced cucumber

Sliced tomato

Half of a lemon, thinly sliced

This is my go-to recipe during a busy week because it's fast, easy, and leaves few dishes to clean up. In 20 minutes, you have a fabulous meal for you and your family!

INSTRUCTIONS

1. Preheat the oven to 400 degrees.

2. Place the salmon fillets skin-side down on a sheet pan. Drizzle the lemon juice and olive oil over the fillets; season with the salt, pepper, and half of the dill; and spread a layer of Dijon Honey Mustard on each fillet.

3. Bake for 15–17 minutes.

4. Once the salmon is cooked, sprinkle on the remaining dill.

5. Spread some extra Dijon Honey Mustard on each roll, add a salmon fillet, and top with lettuce, cucumbers, and tomatoes. Serve with lemon slices on the side and enjoy!

Stuffed *Mushroom* Burger

INGREDIENTS:

Fill It Up!

4 tablespoons extra virgin olive oil

5 teaspoons garlic powder, divided

2 teaspoons salt, divided

2 teaspoons pepper, divided

4 large portobello mushrooms, de-stemmed

10 ounces frozen spinach, defrosted and drained

1 tablespoon fresh sage, chopped

½ cup bread crumbs

4 tablespoons parmesan cheese, shredded

4 scallions, chopped

8 ounces cream cheese, softened

½ teaspoon red pepper flakes

Juice of 1 lemon

Top It Off!

4 burger buns

Beet Ketchup (see page 122 in the condiments section)

4 slices cheddar cheese

INSTRUCTIONS

1. Preheat the oven to 375 degrees.

2. Mix together the olive oil, 2 teaspoons of garlic powder, 1 teaspoon of salt, and 1 teaspoon of pepper. Pour over the mushrooms and allow to marinate for 20 minutes.

3. In a separate bowl, mix together the spinach, sage, bread crumbs, parmesan, scallions, cream cheese, red pepper flakes, lemon juice, 3 teaspoons of garlic powder, 1 teaspoon of salt, and 1 teaspoon of pepper.

4. Place the spinach mixture in the mushrooms.

5. Arrange the stuffed mushrooms on a sheet tray and bake for 20 minutes.

6. Smear each bun with beet ketchup, add a mushroom, and top with a slice of cheese.

MARINATE THOSE MUSHROOMS! Marinating mushrooms is not just for flavor; it also changes the texture. Drizzling on olive oil and letting the mushrooms sit gives a smoother consistency and a beefier taste. I always prepare my mushrooms first so they can marinate while I prepare all my other ingredients and are ready when I am ready to cook.

Tip!

TOFU TO THE RESCUE! Tofu is an awesome busy-week ingredient. It's a blank canvas and cooks very quickly. You can marinate it in dressing, sprinkle on your favorite pantry seasonings, or fry it up in the oven. Fast dinner ingredients = more time to chill out!

Crispy *Tofu* Sandwich

INGREDIENTS:

Fill It Up!

One package (14–16 ounces) firm tofu, drained

4 teaspoons salt, divided

4 teaspoons pepper, divided

4 teaspoons garlic powder, divided

4 teaspoons oregano, divided

1 cup flour

½ cup vegan mayonnaise

1 cup bread crumbs

½ teaspoon red pepper flakes

Top It Off!

Tom's Sriracha Ketchup (see page 120 in the condiments section)

4 hamburger buns

4 slices sharp cheddar cheese

Store-bought coleslaw

INSTRUCTIONS

1. Cut the tofu into four equal pieces.

2. In a small bowl, combine 1 teaspoon each of salt, pepper, garlic powder, and oregano.

3. Coat the tofu in the seasoning mixture and let marinate for 30 minutes on the counter.

4. Place the flour, mayonnaise, and bread crumbs in separate bowls. Season each bowl with 1 teaspoon each of salt, pepper, garlic powder, and oregano. Sprinkle some red pepper flakes into each bowl.

5. Dip each tofu piece into the flour, then the mayonnaise, then the bread crumbs. Repeat and place on a sheet pan.

6. Place the pan in the refrigerator for 20 minutes or overnight. *NOTE: You can skip putting it in the refrigerator, but it helps hold the breading together.*

7. Preheat the oven to 400 degrees.

8. Spray the breaded tofu with cooking spray and bake on the middle rack of the oven for 20 minutes.

9. Squirt some ketchup on the bun, top with crispy tofu, add a slice of cheese, and finish off with a few spoonfuls of coleslaw; enjoy!

INGREDIENTS:

Fill It Up!

2 pounds of large shrimp, peeled, deveined, and de-tailed

3 tablespoons + ¼ cup extra virgin olive oil, divided

1 teaspoon + ¼ teaspoon garlic powder, divided

1 teaspoon + ¼ teaspoon oregano, divided

2 teaspoons salt, divided

1 cucumber, diced

1 pint cherry tomatoes, sliced in half

1 handful mint, chopped

½ of a red onion, finely diced

¼ pound feta cheese, crumbled

½ cup pitless Kalamata olives, chopped

¼ cup red wine vinegar

1 teaspoon pepper

Top It Off!

2 pitas, cut in half

Feta cheese, crumbled

Sheet Pan *Greek* Pita

This is dedicated to Tom. We went to Greece on our honeymoon. The most magical night was being on a boat off the shores of Greece and having someone cook us a shrimp dinner and a Greek salad.

INSTRUCTIONS

1. Preheat the oven to 400 degrees.

2. Mix the shrimp, 3 tablespoons of olive oil, 1 teaspoon of garlic powder, 1 teaspoon of oregano, and 1 teaspoon of salt on a sheet pan.

3. Spread the shrimp out on the sheet pan so it roasts instead of steams. Cook for 10 minutes.

4. In a medium bowl, mix together the cucumber, tomatoes, mint, onions, feta, olives, red wine vinegar, pepper, ¼ cup of olive oil, ¼ teaspoon of garlic powder, ¼ teaspoon of oregano, and 1 teaspoon of salt; let sit for between 30 minutes and overnight.

5. Add some cucumber salad to each pita, followed by some shrimp, and top it off with more cucumber salad. Sprinkle on extra feta cheese and enjoy!

Chapter 3: *Grilled Cheese* Sandwiches

Every bite of grilled cheese is like sunshine and rainbows on a cloudy day! It is easy to make, usually only takes about 4 minutes to cook, and is comfort food happiness after a long day.

People who love to eat are always the best people.
—Julia Child

INGREDIENTS:

Fill It Up!

2 packages (8 ounces each) frozen spinach, defrosted

1 can (14 ounces) artichoke hearts, drained and chopped

2 cups sharp cheddar cheese, grated

2 packages (8 ounces each) cream cheese, softened

4 tablespoons sour cream

1 teaspoon salt

1 teaspoon pepper

1 teaspoon garlic powder

1 teaspoon red pepper flakes

1 teaspoon oregano

Juice of half a lemon

3 scallions, chopped

Top It Off!

Extra Creamy Homemade Mayonnaise (see page 126 in the condiments section)

8 slices sourdough bread

Spinach Artichoke Grilled Cheese

I make the filling for this sandwich on Sunday night and leave it in the refrigerator overnight. When I get home from work on Monday, I'm ready to load up the sandwich. The crunch and cheesy bite of this sandwich is the perfect way to start the week!

INSTRUCTIONS

1. In a large bowl, mix together the spinach, artichoke hearts, cheddar cheese, cream cheese, sour cream, salt, pepper, garlic powder, red pepper flakes, oregano, lemon juice, and scallions.

2. Spread mayonnaise on both sides of each bread slice.

3. Evenly divide the spinach artichoke mixture across the four sandwiches. Add the top slice of bread and place the sandwich in a heated skillet.

4. Cook on medium heat for 3 minutes per side.

MAKE THOSE VEGGIES WORK FOR YOU!

Frozen veggies are cooked and blanched so they keep their color and flavor; they are then flash-frozen at the peak of freshness. It is a huge time-saver so you can use all that freed-up time to chill out and work on YOU!

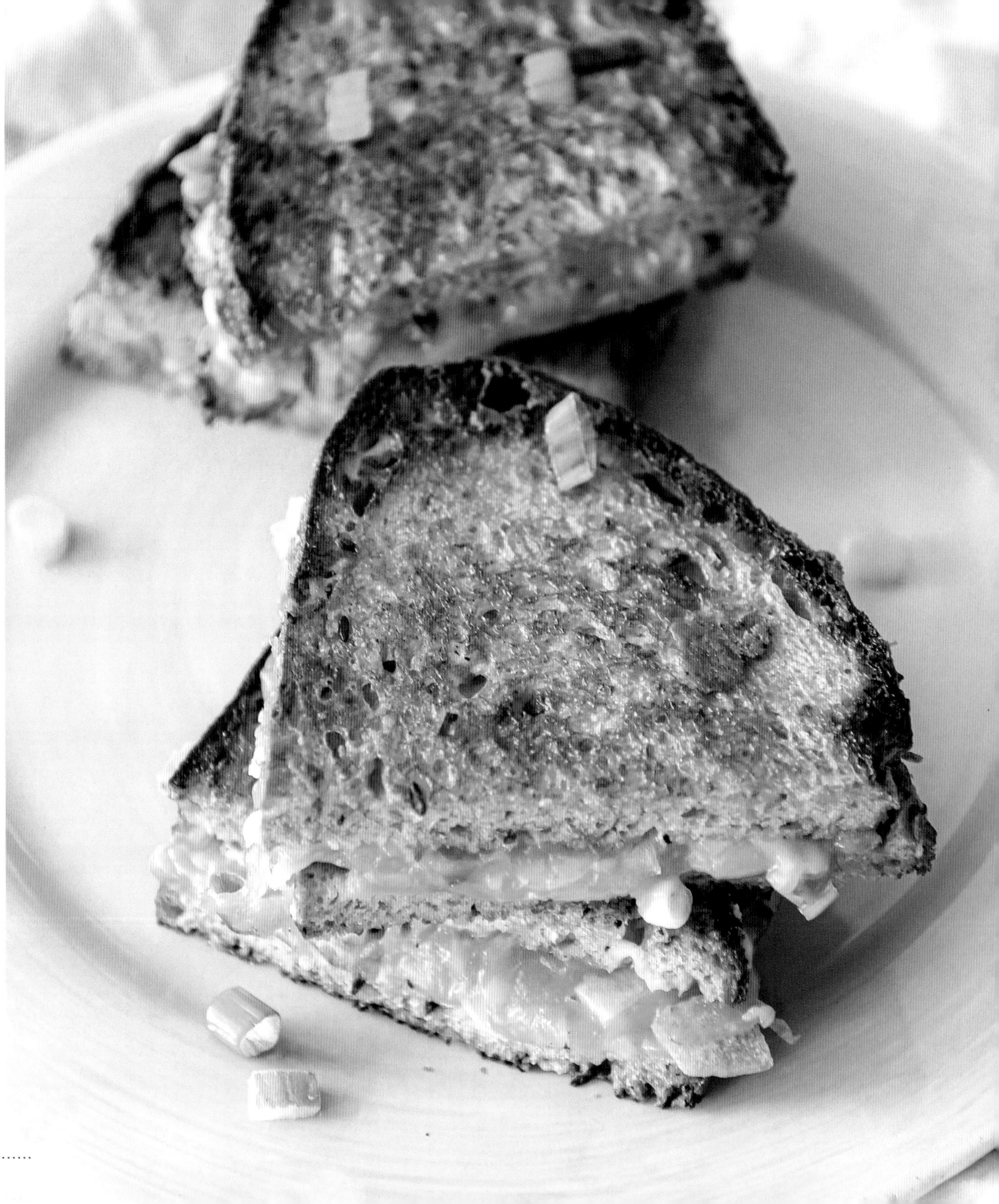

Ultimate *Crunchy* Grilled Cheese

INGREDIENTS:

Fill It Up!

½ of a red onion, finely chopped

4 scallions, chopped

1 cup sharp cheddar cheese, shredded

1 cup gruyère cheese, shredded

1 cup swiss cheese, shredded

Top It Off!

Extra Creamy Homemade Mayonnaise (see page 126 in the condiments section)

8 slices sourdough bread

This is dedicated to my trip to London with my mom and Tom. We went to one of my favorite places in London: Borough Market. There is a stand where they sell toasties (the British name for grilled cheese). It was so simple but so extraordinary! The most amazing part was the crunchy crouton-like outside and creamy, crunchy texture of the inside. They added tiny chopped pieces of red onion. OMG—that made all the difference! This is my version of that amazing culinary moment.

INSTRUCTIONS

1. Mix the onions, scallions, and cheddar, gruyère, and swiss cheeses together in a bowl.

2. Spread mayonnaise on both sides of each bread slice.

3. Divide the cheese mixture evenly across four slices of bread. Close the sandwich and cook on medium heat in a hot skillet for 3 minutes per side. Enjoy!

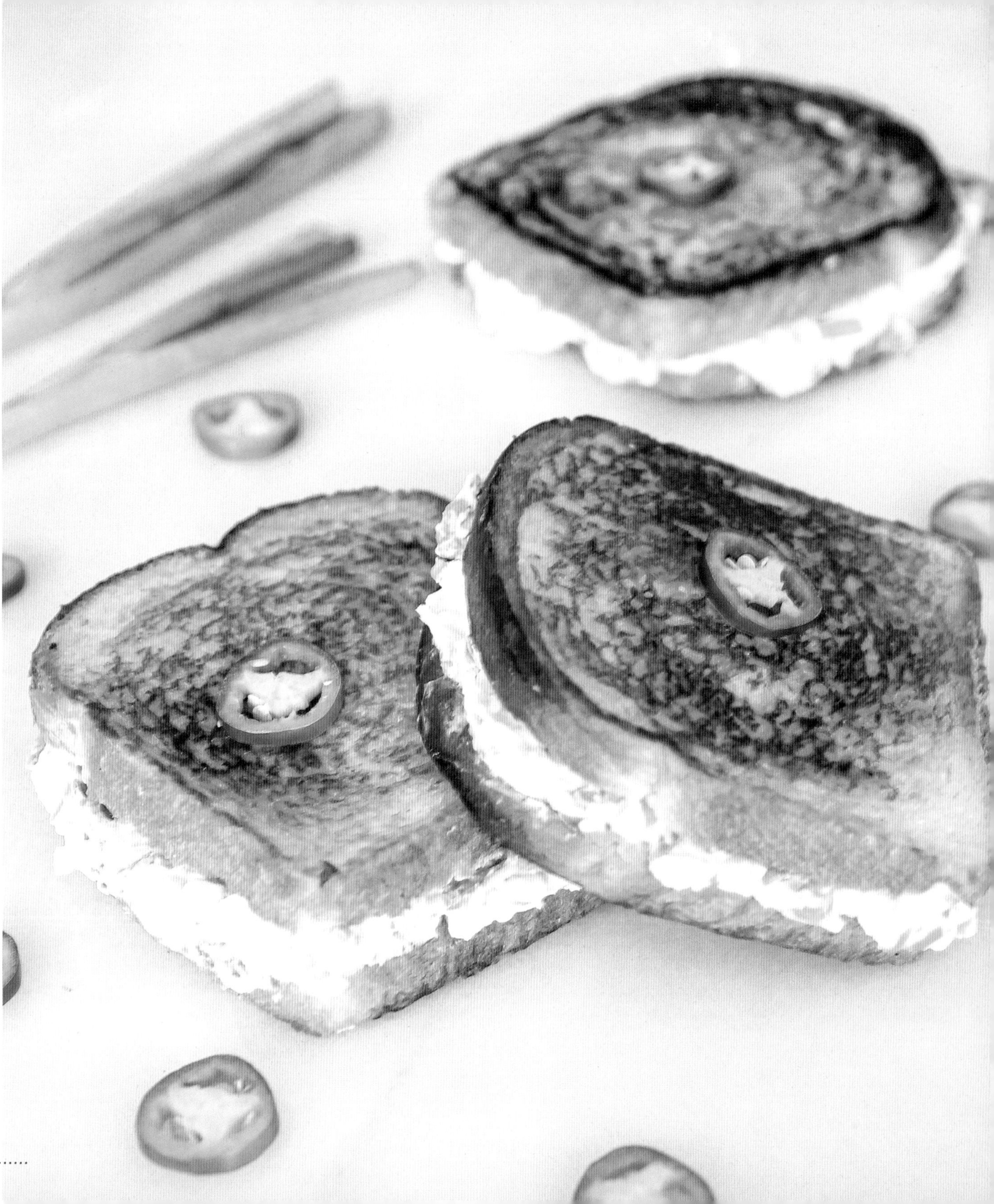

Jalapeño Popper Grilled Cheese

INGREDIENTS:

Fill It Up!

16 ounces cream cheese, softened

2 cups cheddar cheese, shredded

2 jalapeños, deseeded and finely chopped

3 scallions, chopped

1 teaspoon salt

1 teaspoon pepper

1 teaspoon garlic powder

Juice of half a lemon

Top It Off!

8 slices white bread

Extra Creamy Homemade Mayonnaise (see page 126 in the condiments section)

I make the filling for this sandwich on Sunday night and leave it in the refrigerator overnight. When I get home from work on Monday, I'm ready to load up the sandwich. The crunch and cheesy bite of this sandwich is the perfect way to start the week!

INSTRUCTIONS

1. Mix the cream cheese, cheddar cheese, jalapeños, scallions, salt, pepper, garlic powder, and lemon juice together.

2. Split the cheese mixture evenly onto four slices of bread. Add the top piece of bread.

3. Generously spread mayonnaise on the outside of each slice of bread. Cook in a hot pan for 3 minutes per side on medium heat.

"Cooking is one of the greatest gifts
you can give those that you love."
—Ina Garten

INGREDIENTS:

Fill It Up!

2 cups ricotta cheese

1 handful fresh parsley, chopped

10 basil leaves, chopped

1 teaspoon salt

1 teaspoon pepper

½ teaspoon dried oregano

1 teaspoon garlic powder

¼ teaspoon red pepper flakes

4 tablespoons extra virgin olive oil

4 tablespoons parmesan cheese, grated

Top It Off!

8 slices sourdough bread

Extra Creamy Homemade Mayonnaise (see page 126 in the condiments section)

Parmesan cheese, grated

2 cups of your favorite marinara sauce

Calzone Grilled Cheese

Growing up in New Jersey, calzones were my hand pies! My mom would reward me for having an awesome week by getting me a hot calzone oozing with cheese. Celebrate small accomplishments throughout the week and treat yourself to a dinner treat. Don't wait till big holidays to celebrate how far you've come!

INSTRUCTIONS

1. In a large bowl, mix together the ricotta, parsley, basil, salt, pepper, oregano, garlic powder, red pepper flakes, olive oil, and 4 tablespoons of parmesan cheese.

2. Divide the mixture evenly across four slices of bread and top with another slice of bread.

3. Spread lots of mayonnaise on the outside of each bread slice. Cook in a pan for 3 minutes per side on medium heat.

4. While still hot, sprinkle parmesan cheese on both sides of the bread. Dip in warm marinara sauce and enjoy!

Greek
Grilled Cheese

Fill It Up!

¼ cup extra virgin olive oil

Juice of 1 lemon

1 teaspoon pepper

1 teaspoon oregano

1 teaspoon garlic powder

¼ teaspoon red pepper flakes

1 pound feta cheese, cut into eight slices

Top It Off!

8 slices sourdough bread

½ cup fresh dill, chopped

1 large cucumber, thinly sliced

Extra Creamy Homemade Mayonnaise (see page 126 in the condiments section)

1. Mix the oil, lemon juice, pepper, oregano, garlic powder, and red pepper flakes in a bowl to create a vinaigrette.

2. Marinate the feta slices in the vinaigrette for 20 minutes.

3. Place equal amounts of the marinated feta onto four slices of bread. Top with some dill and cucumber slices, followed by the top slice of bread.

4. Spread mayonnaise on the outside of each bread slice. Cook in a hot pan for 3 minutes per side on medium heat.

FETA-TASTIC! Feta provides awesome flavor. It is naturally salty and tangy, so marinating it in olive oil, lemon juice, pepper, oregano, garlic powder, and red pepper flakes enhances its flavor. I do this even when I'm just crumbling feta on my salad. Be sure to let it marinate for at least 20 minutes so the flavor soaks throughout the cheese. You can also marinate the night before so it makes dinner prep easier the day you cook!

"Cooking is the ultimate giving."
—Jamie Oliver

Broccoli *Cheddar* Grilled Cheese

INGREDIENTS:

Fill It Up!

3 bags (10 ounces each) frozen broccoli, defrosted and chopped

1 tablespoon red wine vinegar

2 cups cheddar cheese, shredded

1 teaspoon salt

1 teaspoon pepper

½ teaspoon red pepper flakes

Top It Off!

Extra Creamy Homemade Mayonnaise (see page 126 in the condiments section)

8 slices sourdough bread

INSTRUCTIONS

1. In a large bowl, mix together the broccoli, red wine vinegar, cheddar cheese, salt, pepper, and red pepper flakes.

2. Add some mayonnaise to both sides of each bread slice.

3. Divide the broccoli filling evenly across four slices of bread and finish off each sandwich with the top piece of bread.

4. Cook in a pan on medium heat for 3 minutes on each side. Slightly press down on the sandwich as you cook to help keep it from falling apart.

A TIP FOR FABULOUS MEALS AT HOME!

Add some acidity to your dish. In restaurants, before your dish is served, the chef will usually add some acid to brighten up your food. I always say a squeeze of lemon, dash of vinegar, or shave of chocolate is sunshine on a cloudy day!

Hot Dog Grilled Cheese

INGREDIENTS:

Fill It Up!

8 teaspoons yellow mustard

¼ cup relish

16 slices cheddar cheese

4 hot dogs, cooked and sliced down the middle lengthwise

Top It Off!

Extra Creamy Homemade Mayonnaise (see page 126 in the condiments section)

4 slices white bread

INSTRUCTIONS

1. Spread mayonnaise on one side of each bread slice.

2. Place the bread, mayo-side down, in a pan.

3. Spread mustard and relish on each slice of bread; add four slices of cheese and cook on medium heat for 2 minutes.

4. Add a hot dog to each slice of bread; carefully fold the bread in half and cook each side for another minute, pressing down on the bread with a spatula to help keep the sandwich together. Enjoy!

HOT DOG! To quickly cook the hot dog, you can heat it in a microwave for 50 seconds. Or, if you're feeling adventurous, you can try frying it in the same pan you're cooking the grilled cheese in, just be sure to wipe out the pan with a paper towel before cooking the grilled cheese.

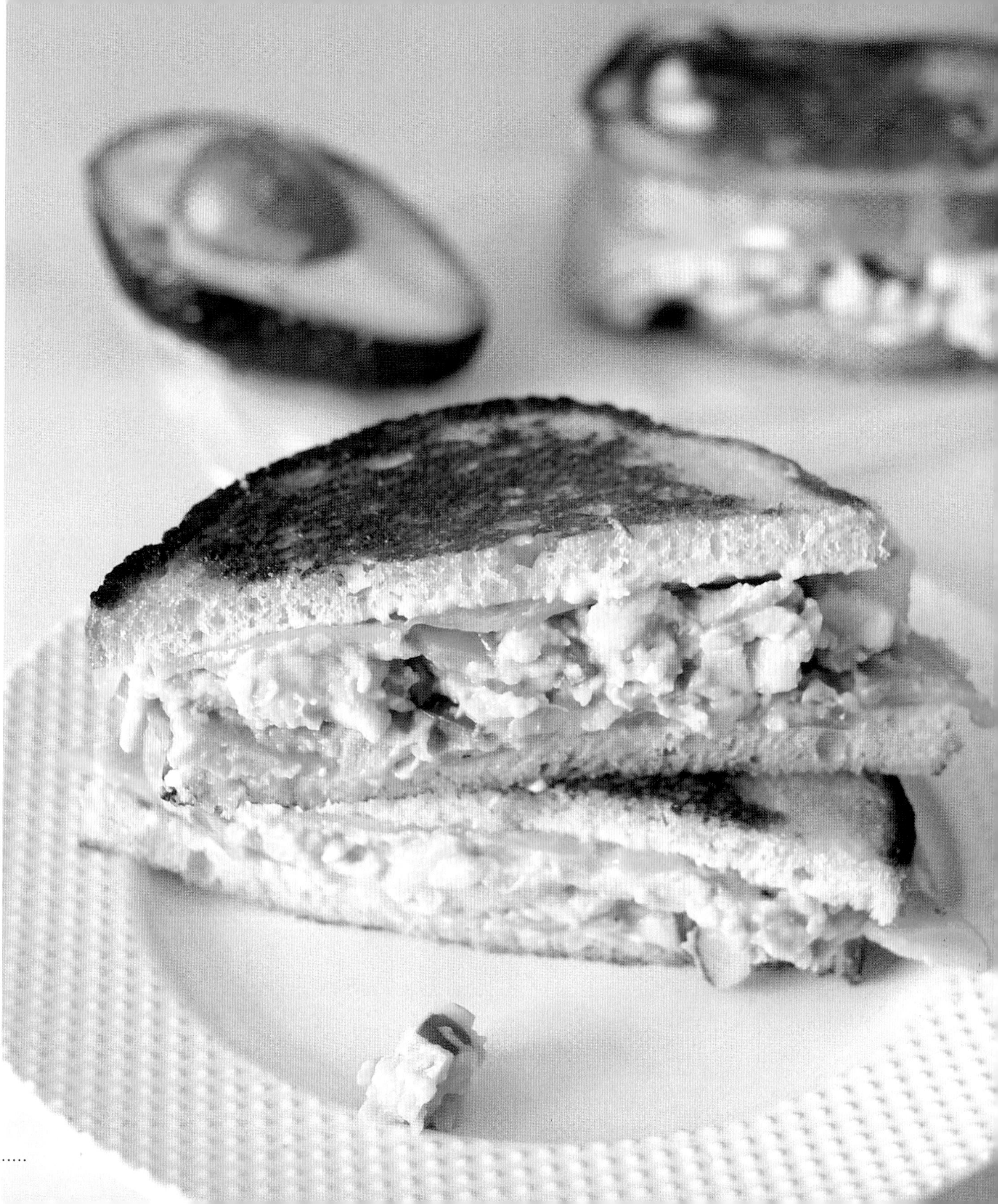

Guacamole Grilled Cheese

INGREDIENTS:

Fill It Up!

3 avocados

One-fourth of a red onion, chopped

1 jalapeño, deseeded

1 handful cilantro, chopped (or you can substitute equal parts parsley and mint)

1 tablespoon apple cider vinegar

Juice of 1 lime

1 teaspoon salt

1 teaspoon pepper

1 teaspoon garlic powder

Top It Off!

Extra Creamy Homemade Mayonnaise (see page 126 in the condiments section)

8 slices sourdough bread

16 slices cheddar cheese

INSTRUCTIONS

1. Cut each avocado in half and remove the pits. Scoop out the flesh into a small bowl and mash.

2. Mix together the onion, jalapeño, cilantro, apple cider vinegar, lime juice, salt, pepper, and garlic powder in a small bowl.

3. Add the onion mixture to the avocados and mix well.

4. Spread mayonnaise on both sides of each bread slice.

5. Add two slices of cheese each to four slices of bread, then divide the guacamole into four equal portions and scoop it onto the bread. Top each sandwich with two more slices of cheese and the top piece of bread.

6. Cook in a pan for 3 minutes per side on medium heat.

SEASON WITH CITRUS! Want a tip for extra flavorful guacamole and keeping the vibrant green color? Lots of citrus makes all the difference in flavor and color! But lime isn't the only citrus you can use; add a splash of any vinegar. It not only makes the guacamole taste citrusy, but it is also a strong antioxidant to help keep the avocados from turning brown.

"One cannot think well,
love well, and sleep well
if one has not dined well."
—Virginia Woolf

Lobster Gruyere Grilled Cheese

INGREDIENTS:

Fill It Up!

3 tablespoons butter, melted

1 teaspoon dijon mustard

1 teaspoon salt

1 teaspoon pepper

1 teaspoon dill, chopped

2 scallions, finely chopped

1 pound lobster, cooked and chopped

2 cups gruyère cheese, shredded

Top It Off!

Extra Creamy Homemade Mayonnaise (see page 126 in the condiments section)

8 slices sourdough bread

INSTRUCTIONS

1. Mix the butter, dijon, salt, pepper, dill, and scallions together in a large bowl.

2. Mix in the lobster and gruyère cheese.

3. Spread generous amount of mayonnaise on both sides of each bread slice.

4. Divide the lobster mixture evenly across four slices of bread and add the top piece of bread to each sandwich.

5. Cook in a pan for 3 minutes per side on medium heat.

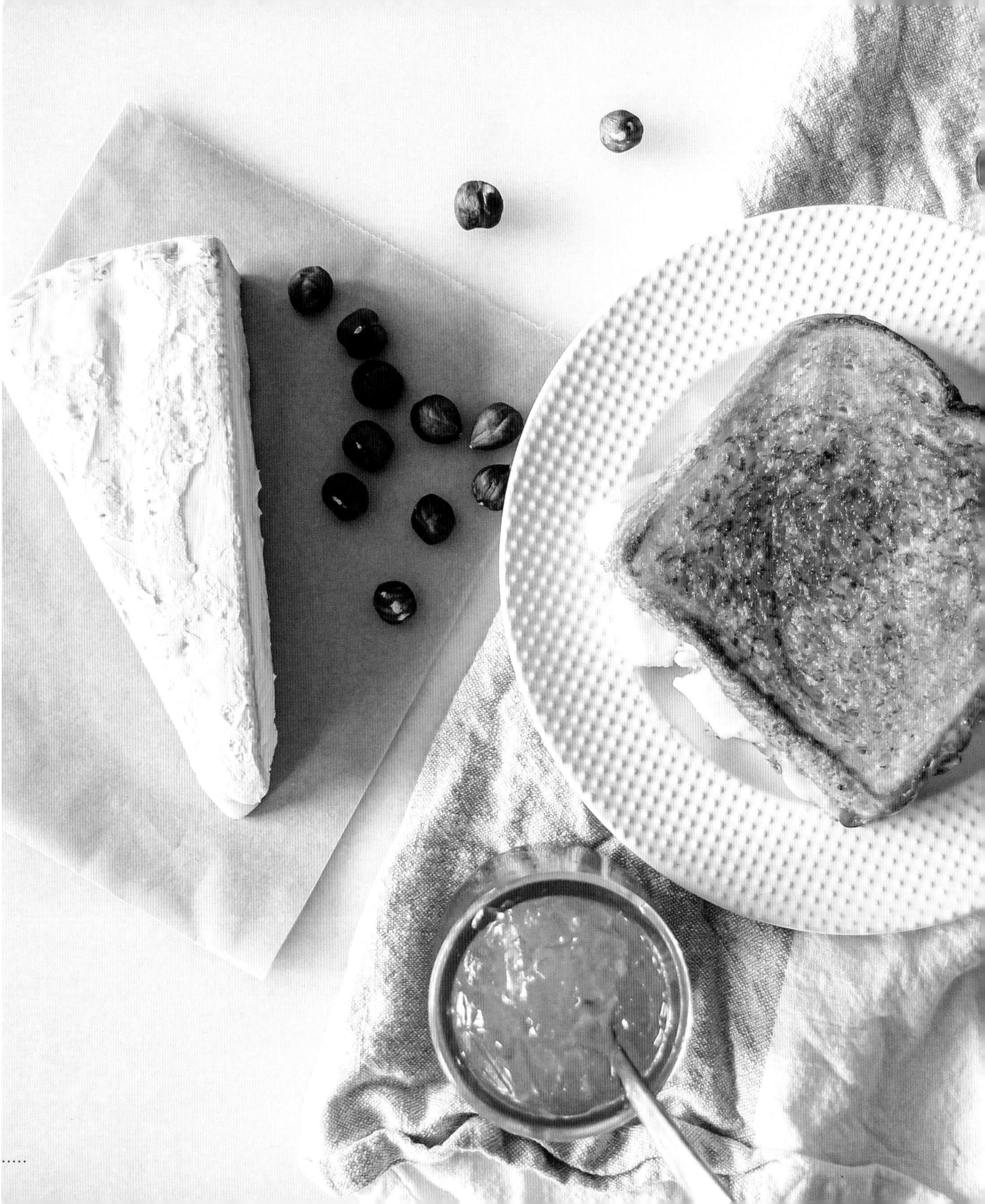

Brie & Apricot Jam Grilled Cheese

INGREDIENTS:

Fill It Up!

8 tablespoons apricot or orange jam

¼ cup chopped roasted hazelnuts

1 wheel double cream brie, sliced

Top It Off!

Extra Creamy Homemade Mayonnaise (see page 126 in the condiments section)

8 slices sourdough bread

Just like life, food needs balance. The salty, pungent cheese of this recipe pairs nicely with the sweet jam. This makes the grilled cheese decadent and light at the same time!

INSTRUCTIONS

1. Spread mayonnaise on both sides of each bread slice.

2. Spread some jam on one side of each slice of bread, then sprinkle chopped hazelnuts onto the jam.

3. Lay some brie slices on the bread, fanning them out to cover the slice. Place another slice of bread on top.

4. Cook in a pan on medium heat for 3 minutes per side.

Chapter 4: *No-Cook* Sandwiches

Sometimes dinner can be even happier when there is so little work, you don't even need to cook a thing! No cooking = happy bites!

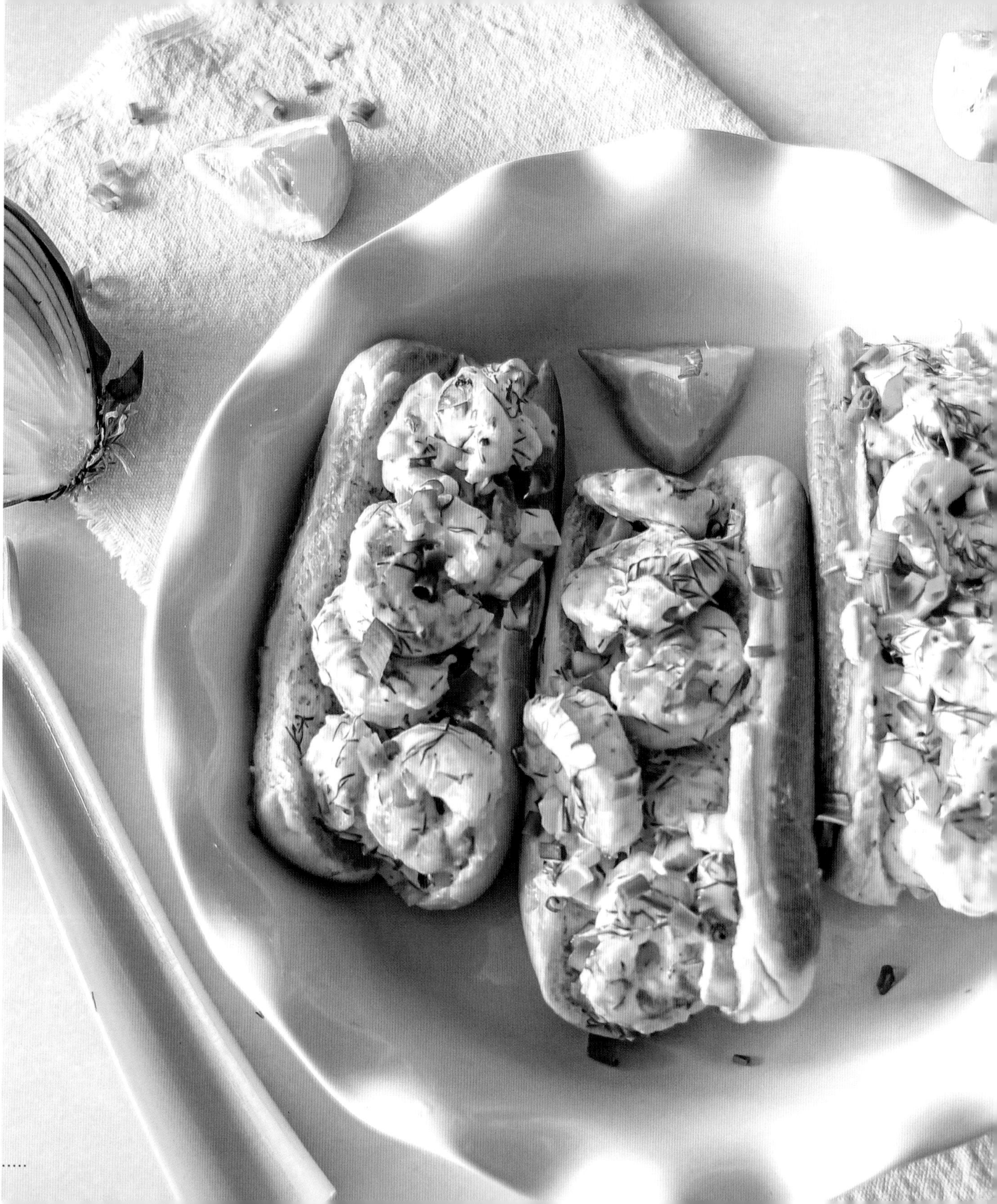

Garlic Dill Shrimp Salad

INGREDIENTS:

Fill It Up!

5 tablespoons mayonnaise

1 celery stalk, finely chopped

One-fourth of a red onion, chopped

2 cloves of garlic, grated

1 handful dill

1 tablespoon apple cider vinegar

1 teaspoon salt

1 teaspoon pepper

Juice of half a lemon

¼ teaspoon red pepper flakes

1 pound shrimp, cooked

Top It Off!

4 hot dog buns, toasted

Lettuce

This recipe is dedicated to Lisa! When you have someone who is both working toward your dreams and has become a great friend, you want to feed them to say thanks! This recipe is one of her faves that I have made for her, and I want to dedicate it to her because without her, this book would not be possible! Thank you for being amazing!

INSTRUCTIONS

1. In a large bowl, combine the mayonnaise, celery, onion, garlic, dill, apple cider vinegar, salt, pepper, lemon juice, and red pepper flakes.

2. Mix in the shrimp.

3. Fill each bun with lettuce and shrimp salad. Enjoy!

COOKING TIP! Buy frozen cooked shrimp from your usual grocery store. This is cheaper than purchasing from fish stores. Just let the shrimp sit in a bowl of cold water for 15 minutes and then pat dry. This makes for easy defrosting! This also works for raw shrimp.

INGREDIENTS:

Fill It Up!

2 cans (15.5 ounces each) chickpeas

2 teaspoons salt, divided

2 teaspoons pepper, divided

½ cup Greek yogurt or vegan mayonnaise

1 teaspoon garlic powder

1 tablespoon hot sauce

1 teaspoon apple cider vinegar

Juice of half a lemon

½ of a red onion, chopped

3 celery stalks, finely chopped

1 handful parsley

Top It Off!

Greek yogurt or vegan mayonnaise

8 slices white bread

Lettuce

Sliced tomato

Blue cheese, crumbled

Buffalo *Chickpea* Sandwich

Chickpea salad is a perfect meal-prep ingredient. Unlike tuna, it can stay in the refrigerator all day without smelling it up! I make a big batch of this salad and eat it all week for dinner.

INSTRUCTIONS

1. Smash the chickpeas to a chunky tuna consistency with 1 teaspoon of salt and 1 teaspoon of pepper.

2. Add the Greek yogurt, garlic powder, hot sauce, apple cider vinegar, lemon juice, onion, celery, parsley, 1 teaspoon of salt, and 1 teaspoon of pepper to the bowl and mix with the chickpeas.

3. Spread extra Greek yogurt on one side of each slice of bread and add the chickpea salad; top with lettuce, tomato, and blue cheese. Enjoy!

Ceviche
Scallop Roll

INGREDIENTS:

Fill It Up!

Juice of 2 limes

Juice of 2 lemons

1 jalapeño, deseeded and chopped

½ cup dill, chopped

1 cucumber, finely chopped

3 tablespoons extra virgin olive oil

One-fourth of a red onion, chopped

1 teaspoon salt

1 teaspoon pepper

¼ teaspoon garlic powder

1½ pounds bay scallops, raw

Top It Off!

Lettuce

4 hot dog buns

INSTRUCTIONS

1. In a large bowl, mix together the lime juice, lemon juice, jalapeño, dill, cucumber, olive oil, onion, salt, pepper, and garlic powder.

2. Add the scallops to the large bowl, mix to coat, and marinate in the refrigerator for 4 hours.

3. Add lettuce to each hot dog bun, along with a scoop of the scallop ceviche.

WHAT SCALLOPS TO BUY! There are two types of scallops: wet scallops and dry scallops. Wet scallops are soaked in preservatives so they last longer. Dry scallops are direct from the fisherman to you! You want to use dry scallops because they taste sweet and fresh. Also, they are all-natural with no chemicals. You can find them at the supermarket—just look at the label or ask at the fish counter.

> "Let food be thy medicine
> and medicine be thy food."
> —Hippocrates

Dijon *Lobster* Salad Sandwich

INGREDIENTS:

Fill It Up!

1 tablespoon regular dijon mustard

1 tablespoon country (grainy) dijon mustard

2 cloves of garlic, grated or finely chopped

¼ teaspoon red pepper flakes

Juice of half a lemon

1 tablespoon white wine vinegar

½ cup extra virgin olive oil

½ cup fresh dill, roughly chopped

1 pound lobster, cooked

2 celery stalks, finely chopped

One-fourth of a red onion, chopped

Top It Off!

4 hot dog buns, toasted

INSTRUCTIONS

1. In a small bowl, mix together the regular and country dijon mustards, garlic, red pepper flakes, lemon juice, white wine vinegar, olive oil, and dill.

2. In a separate bowl, mix together the lobster, celery, onion, and 3–4 tablespoons of the mustard dressing. *NOTE: Use leftover dressing as a marinade, salad dressing, or dip.*

3. Divide the lobster mixture evenly onto each hot dog bun and enjoy.

MAKE-AHEAD SALAD TIP! I always prepare salad ingredients separately from the dressing. This way, if you are having people over, you can make the dressing in advance. This makes less work and you can enjoy your guests instead of spending more time in the kitchen.

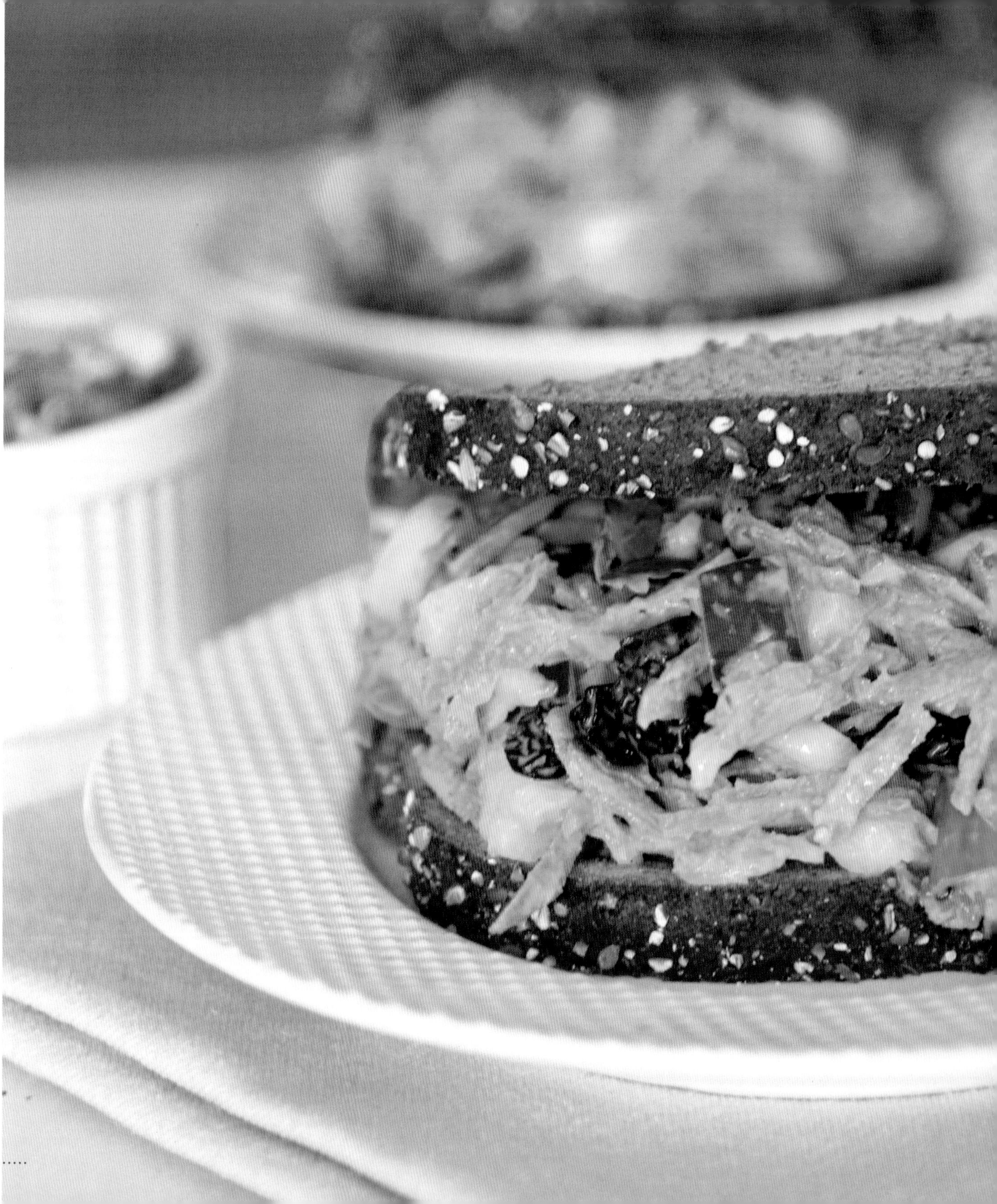

Jewish *Carrot* Salad Sandwich

INGREDIENTS:

Fill It Up!

½ cup fresh pineapple, divided

½ cup Greek yogurt or vegan mayonnaise

1 tablespoon apple cider vinegar

1 teaspoon salt

1 teaspoon pepper

½ teaspoon red pepper flakes

1 teaspoon garlic powder

½ cup raisins

4 cups grated carrots

1 large red onion, chopped

1 handful mint, chopped

½ cup roasted peanuts

Top It Off!

Greek yogurt or vegan mayonnaise

8 slices seeded or multigrain bread

This is a perfect vegetarian or vegan side for friends or family! First, you can totally make this up to 3 days in advance. Second, the sweet carrots and the creamy mayonnaise make this so decadent, everyone will love it!

INSTRUCTIONS

1. Smash ¼ cup pineapple with a fork or potato masher. Chop the remaining ¼ cup in small pieces and set aside.

2. In a large bowl, combine the smashed pineapple, Greek yogurt, apple cider vinegar, salt, pepper, red pepper flakes, garlic powder, and raisins.

3. Add the carrots to the large bowl and mix well.

4. Gently fold in the chunks of pineapple, onion, and mint. Let sit in the refrigerator for a couple of hours or, for best results, overnight.

5. Mix in the peanuts.

6. Slather extra Greek yogurt on one side of each slice of bread. Pile on some carrot salad and top with another slice of bread. Enjoy!

FRESHLY GRATED! I always say grate your own veggies, especially carrots. When you buy pre-grated, they lose moisture and flavor. When you get whole carrots home from the store, grate them and cover with a wet cloth. This will help keep them fresh for days!

INGREDIENTS:

Fill It Up!

1 1-pound bag roasted salted peanuts

2 tablespoons extra virgin olive oil

1 tablespoon honey

1 teaspoon ground cinnamon

⅛ teaspoon nutmeg

⅛ teaspoon cayenne pepper (optional)

1 pear

Juice of half a lemon

Top It Off!

4 slices sourdough bread

Honey

¼ cup pomegranate seeds

1 handful mint, chopped

Open-Face Homemade Peanut Butter & Pear Sandwich

Sometimes something looks hard to make, but it is surprisingly easy. It's all about perspective and trying new things. The possibilities are amazing! This recipe is a great culinary example. Homemade peanut butter is just placing ingredients in a blender and you're done. I hope this inspires you to try new things!

INSTRUCTIONS

1. Put the peanuts in a blender and blend until it looks like peanut sand.

2. Add the olive oil, honey, cinnamon, nutmeg, and cayenne pepper; blend until it reaches a peanut butter texture.

3. Cut the pear into thin slices; squeeze the lemon juice on the pears to help keep them from browning.

4. Spread lots of the peanut butter mixture on each slice of bread.

5. Add slices of pear to each sandwich and generously drizzle on some honey, toss on some pomegranate seeds, and sprinkle on some mint. Enjoy!

Burrata *Pesto Caprese* Sandwich

INGREDIENTS:

Fill It Up!

¼ cup extra virgin olive oil

½ teaspoon dried oregano

½ teaspoon garlic powder

¼ teaspoon red pepper flakes

2 beefsteak tomatoes, cut into thick slices

4 medium pieces of burrata

Top It Off!

4 mini brioche rolls

Arugula Pesto (see page 124 in the condiments section)

This is dedicated to Tom. He loves burrata! If it's on the menu, he will always order it! It's always great when food makes the people you love happy. Cheers to the people we love!

INSTRUCTIONS

1. Into the middle of each roll, cut out a hollow that goes about half-way down; reserve the cut-out top.

2. In a small bowl, combine the olive oil, oregano, garlic powder, and red pepper flakes.

3. Brush the oil into the bread hollows.

4. Place a slice of tomato into each hollow and brush with the oil.

5. Add one burrata piece to each roll.

6. Pour 1–2 teaspoons of pesto over the burrata and add the top piece of the roll; enjoy! *Warning: messy, cheesy fun ahead!*

“*The people who give you their food give you their heart.*”
—Cesar Chavez

Chips & Dip Sandwich

This is your treat-yourself-because-you-are-fabulous sandwich. Even though being an adult comes with lots of responsibilities, there is always time to be silly and decadent! When life gets tough, smash some chips and dip between two slices of bread and take a break from your worries. Just hear the crunch and know it will be okay!

INGREDIENTS:

Fill It Up!

1 bag ridged potato chips

1 cup blue cheese dip

Top It Off!

Mayonnaise

8 slices white bread

INSTRUCTIONS

1. Slather mayo on each slice of bread.

2. Layer the bread with lots of chips.

3. Pour some blue cheese dip all over the chips and then top with another bread slice.

4. Smoosh the sandwich a tiny bit to help keep the insides in.

INGREDIENTS:

Fill It Up!

¼ cup vodka

1 ½ pounds wild-caught salmon

¼ cup salt

½ teaspoon black pepper

⅓ cup sugar

Zest of 1 orange

Zest of 1 lemon

1 handful fresh dill, divided

3 tablespoons everything bagel seasoning

Top It Off!

Scallion cream cheese, softened

4 bagels

4 slices beefsteak tomatoes

Chopped dill

Chopped red onion

Homemade Everything-Bagel Lox on a Bagel

This has been my weekend brunch since I was a kid. My dad and I would go to the bagel store for hot, fresh bagels right out of the oven. This was a fun family tradition! The perfect way to stay grounded and filled with gratitude is to have a weekly foodie tradition. Eating, laughing, and being together is the best medicine for a long week!

INSTRUCTIONS

1. Pour the vodka evenly over both sides of the salmon.

2. In a small bowl, mix together the salt, pepper, sugar, orange zest, and lemon zest.

3. Rub the salt mixture onto both sides of the salmon.

4. Lay half of the dill on the bottom of a casserole dish and place the salmon on the dill.

5. Cover the top of the salmon with the other half of the dill.

6. Wrap the dish with plastic wrap and leave in the refrigerator for 3 days.

7. Take the salmon out of the refrigerator. Rinse it thoroughly with water and pat dry.

8. Sprinkle the everything bagel seasoning over the salmon and then slice thin.

9. Add cream cheese to a bagel. Lay on some homemade lox, add a slice of tomato on top, and sprinkle with some dill and onions.

Arugula *Pesto Tuna Salad* Sandwich

INGREDIENTS:

Fill It Up!

Juice of half a lemon

½ cup Arugula Pesto (see page 124 in the condiments section)

½ cup Extra Creamy Homemade Mayonnaise (see page 126 in the condiments section)

2 cans (5 ounces each) tuna, drained

¼ of a red onion, chopped finely

Top It Off!

Extra Creamy Homemade Mayonnaise

8 slices white bread

4 slices tomato

INSTRUCTIONS

1. In a large bowl, mix together the lemon juice, pesto, and mayonnaise.

2. Add the tuna and onion.

3. Put in the refrigerator for a few hours or overnight.

4. Add lots of mayo to each slice of bread and top with some tuna salad. Add a tomato slice and the top slice of bread; enjoy!

LEMON, LEMON, LEMON! The tip to great tasting tuna is lemon! I like to mix all my ingredients together and then squeeze lots of lemon on top. Because tuna can be salty, the lemon brightens up the dish and is like sunshine on a cloudy day!

Chapter 5: *No Bread* Sandwiches

Get ready for some easy sandwiches with fun culinary top hats instead of bread!

The only time to eat diet food is while you're waiting for the steak to cook.
—Julia Child

Potato *Latkes* Sandwich (NJ Sloppy Joe)

No one makes better latkes than my mom! They are the best, but they are an all-day process. So I make them with mashed potatoes instead. No more peeling potatoes because I use buttery Yukon Gold potatoes. You can either follow my recipe below, buy your favorite mashed potatoes and start at step 6, or buy prepared latkes and jump straight to assembling your sandwich with step 11. I just love making life easier in the kitchen so you have more time with your family!

INGREDIENTS:

Fill It Up!

1 pound turkey slices

Top It Off!

8 Mashed Potato Latkes (see recipe below) or store-bought latkes

Mama Goldstein's Russian Dressing (see page 121 in the condiments section)

4 slices swiss cheese

1 cup store-bought coleslaw

Mashed Potato Latkes

3 pounds Yukon Gold potatoes, cut in half

4 cloves of garlic, crushed

4 cups chicken stock

2 teaspoons salt, divided

Chives to taste, chopped

3 tablespoons butter

4 scallions, chopped

1 teaspoon pepper

1 egg

3 tablespoons vegetable oil

INSTRUCTIONS

1. Place the potatoes in a pot with the garlic, chicken stock, and 1 teaspoon of salt.

2. Turn the stove on high; bring to a boil and continue cooking for 15 minutes.

3. Drain the potatoes when they are soft and can be easily pierced with a knife.

4. Place the potatoes back in the hot pot, add the chives, and mash well.

5. Once mashed, add the butter, scallions, pepper, and 1 teaspoon of salt. Mix to combine and then let the potatoes cool.

6. Once cooled, mix an egg into the potatoes.

7. Form eight equal-sized patties out of the potato mixture.

8. Pour the oil into a non-stick pan and heat to medium.

9. Working in batches, place the patties in the hot oil. Fry approximately 2 minutes per side.

10. Remove from the pan, drain on a paper towel, and salt while hot!

11. Top a latke with some Russian dressing, then some turkey and a slice of cheese, followed by a heaping mound of coleslaw.

12. Drizzle on more Russian dressing and then top with another latke; enjoy!

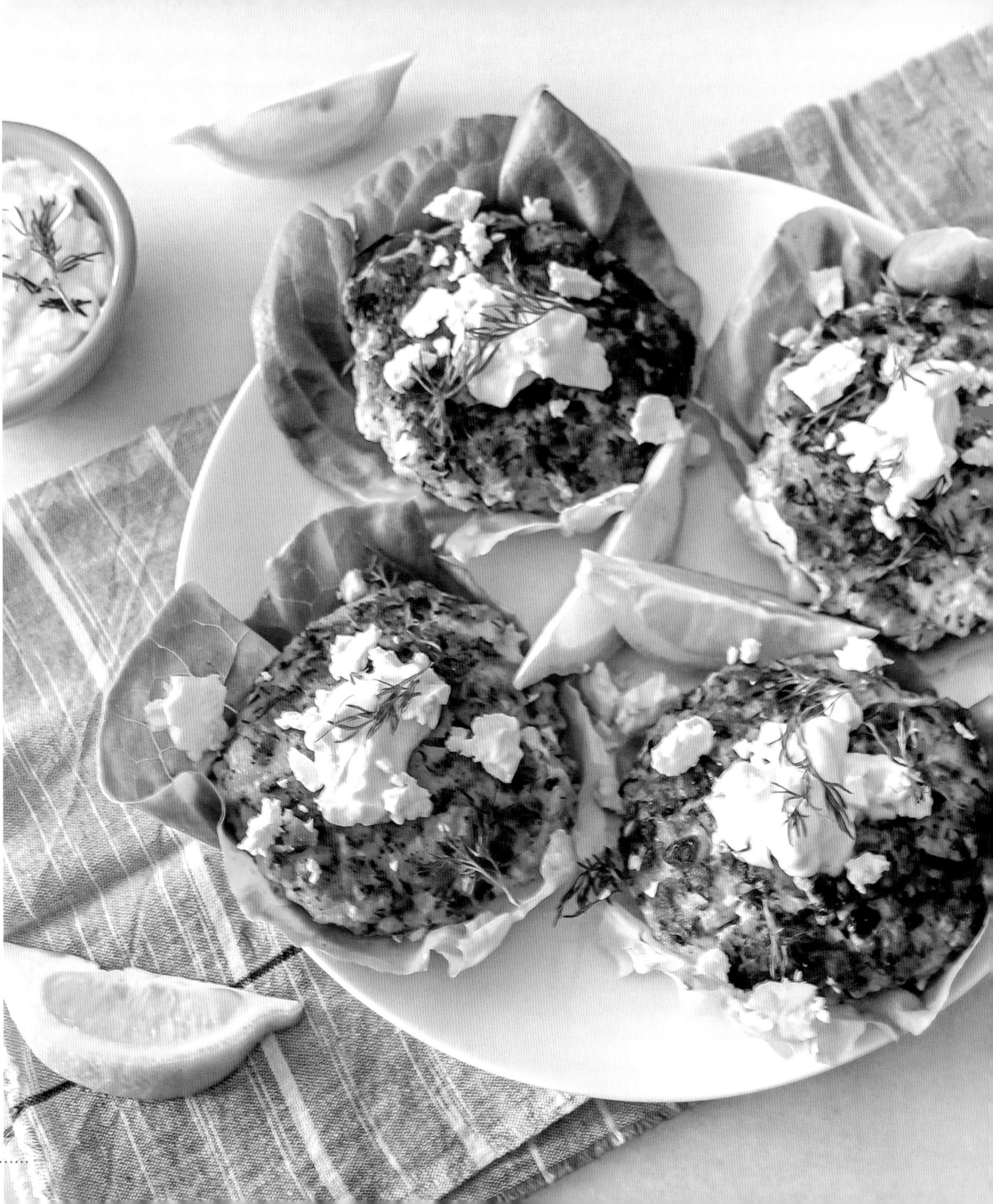

Shrimp Burger with Lettuce Bun

INGREDIENTS:

Fill It Up!

1 ½ pounds shrimp, raw, peeled, deveined, and no tail

1 teaspoon salt

1 teaspoon pepper

1 handful dill

1 clove of garlic, chopped

2 scallions, chopped

½ teaspoon red pepper flakes

1 teaspoon oregano

1 egg

½ cup panko bread crumbs

¼ cup feta cheese, crumbled

Juice of 1 lemon, divided

4 tablespoons mayonnaise

Top It Off!

large romaine lettuce leaves, each shaped into a cup

Feta cheese, crumbled

INSTRUCTIONS

1. In a food processor, combine the shrimp, salt, pepper, dill, garlic, scallions, red pepper flakes, oregano, egg, panko, feta, and one half of the lemon juice; pulse to a chunky paste.

2. In a small bowl, mix together the mayonnaise, the remaining half of the lemon juice, a pinch of salt, and a pinch of pepper; set aside.

3. Form the shrimp meat into four patties. Cook in a pan with oil on medium heat for 5 minutes, flipping halfway through.

4. Place a burger into each lettuce cup, then add some feta, drizzle on some of the prepared dressing, and enjoy!

MAKE IT THE NIGHT BEFORE! Shrimp burgers are a perfect make-ahead meal. You can blend all the ingredients in a bowl the night before; just leave out the lemon and mix it in when you're ready to cook (otherwise the citrus will start to cook the shrimp!). When you get home from work, all you have to do is form the patties and cook for 5 minutes and then dinner is done!

*"Food is symbolic of love
when words are inadequate."
— Alan D. Wolfelt*

NYC *Deli Pickle* Sandwich

INGREDIENTS:

Fill It Up!

½ pound pastrami

Top It Off!

4 extra-large pickles, sliced in half lengthwise

Mama Goldstein's Russian Dressing (see page 121 in the condiments section)

4 slices swiss cheese

This recipe is your culinary trip to New York City! Pastrami with Russian dressing and a pickle on the side is an iconic NYC sandwich. Using pickles as the bread adds a juicy, crunchy component to the sandwich. Also, it's great for your low carb friends!

INSTRUCTIONS

1. Hollow out each pickle slice.

2. Place four pickle halves on a plate and add some Russian dressing into each hollow.

3. To the remaining four pickle halves, layer on some pastrami, swiss cheese, and Russian dressing.

4. Pair off the pickle halves to complete the sandwich. Enjoy!

Leftover Grilled Chicken BLT Club

INGREDIENTS:

Fill It Up!

8 slices bacon, cooked

Lettuce slices

Tomato slices

Top It Off!

Tom's Sriracha Ketchup (see page 120 in the condiments section)

4 grilled chicken breasts, cut in half

½ pound blue cheese, cut into four slices

INSTRUCTIONS

1. Spread some sriracha ketchup on four halves of the chicken breasts.

2. Top with bacon, lettuce, tomato, and a slice of blue cheese.

3. Finish it off with the other half of the grilled chicken and enjoy!

DOUBLE THE TIPS, DOUBLE THE DELICIOUSNESS! Make life easier and turn leftovers into the new star of the show! When you grill chicken, make double. You can then freeze half to make this sandwich on a busy weekday! Also, cook your bacon on a sheet pan. This way you get even cooking and crispy results; plus, no greasy mess from frying the bacon.

"*A balanced diet is a cookie in each hand.*"
—*Barbara Johnson*

Cheesy Grilled Peach Sandwich

INGREDIENTS:

Fill It Up!

4 slices prosciutto

4 tablespoons honey

Top It Off!

4 peaches, cut in half and seeded

4 ounces goat cheese

Honey

¼ teaspoon black pepper

1 handful mint, chopped

INSTRUCTIONS

1. Preheat the oven to 400 degrees.

2. Brush olive oil on the cut side of the peach and season with salt and pepper.

3. Grill peaches cut-side down for 1 minute or so till you get grill marks.

4. Place prosciutto on a sheet tray and cook in the preheated oven for 15 minutes or until crispy.

5. Brush 4 tablespoons of honey over the prosciutto while it is still hot.

6. Start assembling the sandwich with a peach half cut-side up. Smear with goat cheese, drizzle with honey, and add pepper. Top with mint and prosciutto. Add the other half of the peach, cut side down, and enjoy!

Tip!

HOW TO PICK THE PERFECT PEACH! The firmer the peach, the fresher it is. You want a slightly soft yet still firm peach, and when you smell it, it should smell sweet.

Fried *Eggplant* Parm

INGREDIENTS:

Fill It Up!

1 jar of your favorite marinara sauce

10 basil leaves, chopped

4 slices mozzarella cheese

Top It Off!

1 cup flour

3 eggs

1 cup panko bread crumbs

2 teaspoons salt

3 teaspoons pepper

3 teaspoons garlic powder

3 teaspoons oregano

3 teaspoon red pepper flakes

¼ cup parmesan cheese, grated

Small eggplant

INSTRUCTIONS

1. Place the flour, egg, and panko on three separate plates.

2. Season each plate with 1 teaspoon each of salt, pepper, garlic powder, oregano, and red pepper flakes.

3. Add the parmesan to the panko and mix to combine.

4. Cut the eggplant into eight slices; salt and pepper each slice.

5. Coat each eggplant slice with the flour, then egg, then panko.

6. In a pan with ¼-inch of oil, fry both sides of the eggplant slices on medium heat for approximately 2 minutes or until brown.

7. Once brown, remove the eggplant slices from the pan and sprinkle with a little salt while they're still hot.

8. Top a slice of fried eggplant with a couple tablespoons of marinara, some basil, and a slice of mozzarella; finish off with another slice of eggplant and enjoy!

SEASON EVERYTHING! If you season every layer, you have a better chance to taste flavor throughout the dish as you bite down. If you only season the outside layer, then the inside will be bland. You can use this rule for all your cooking!

College Days
Inside-Out
Breakfast Sandwich

INGREDIENTS:

Fill It Up!

2 tablespoons butter, divided

7 eggs, whisked in a bowl

1 heaping tablespoon sour cream

1 bunch chives, chopped

1 teaspoon salt

1 teaspoon pepper

Top It Off!

1½ pounds breakfast sausage, raw and formed into eight patties

2 tablespoons extra virgin olive oil

Tom's Sriracha Ketchup (see page 120 in the condiments section)

4 slices cheddar cheese

INSTRUCTIONS

1. Cook the sausage patties on medium high heat in a pan with the olive oil for 4 minutes per side. Once cooked, pat dry and set aside.

2. Drain the pan and put on low heat with 1 tablespoon of butter. Whisk in the eggs and cook on low, mixing until they become wet scrambled eggs.

3. Shut off the heat and add the sour cream, chives, salt, pepper, and 1 tablespoon of butter. Mix to combine.

4. Place a sausage patty on a plate. Spread some sriracha ketchup on the sausage; top with scrambled eggs and a slice of cheese. Then top another sausage patty with ketchup and place on the top of your sandwich. Cheers to brunch!

 Tip!

PERFECT SCRAMBLED EGG TIPS! First, do not salt the eggs until they're cooked. The salt draws out water and will make a less fluffy egg. Second, cook the eggs on low heat. If you cook the eggs on high heat, they will become rubbery and tough. When the eggs look like wet curds, shut off the heat and let the eggs continue to cook. This will make the eggs super creamy!

"You know, food is such a hug for people."
—Rachael Ray

Spicy Sushi Sandwich

INGREDIENTS:

Fill It Up!

½ cup mayonnaise

Juice of 1 lime

2 tablespoons Tom's Sriracha Ketchup (see page 120 in the condiments section)

½ pound sushi-grade tuna

1 teaspoon salt

1 teaspoon pepper

2 scallions, chopped

Top It Off!

2 scallions, finely chopped

3 cups sushi rice or sticky rice, cooked

2 tablespoons rice wine vinegar

1 cucumber, sliced thin

Toasted sesame seeds

INSTRUCTIONS

1. In a large bowl, mix together the mayonnaise, lime juice, and sriracha ketchup.

2. Add the tuna, salt, pepper, and chopped scallions to the large bowl; mix to combine.

3. Place in the refrigerator to marinate for at least an hour, after which you can add more sriracha ketchup (for a little more heat) or more mayonnaise (if you want a creamier finish).

4. Mix the finely chopped scallions together with the cooked rice and rice wine vinegar.

5. Form eight patties out of the rice and put in the refrigerator for between 1 hour and overnight.

6. Brush olive oil on both sides of each rice patty and cook for 3 minutes per side on medium high heat in a pan.

7. Remove from the heat and layer some thin cucumber slices on the bottom rice bun; top with some of the tuna mixture and sprinkle on some toasted sesame seeds. Add more cucumber and top with another rice patty. Sprinkle some more toasted sesames on top. Enjoy!

SO MANY OPTIONS! You can make this vegetarian! Mix the spicy sauce with avocado, cucumbers, or even salad greens. Also, if you don't want raw fish, you can use smoked salmon in place of the tuna!

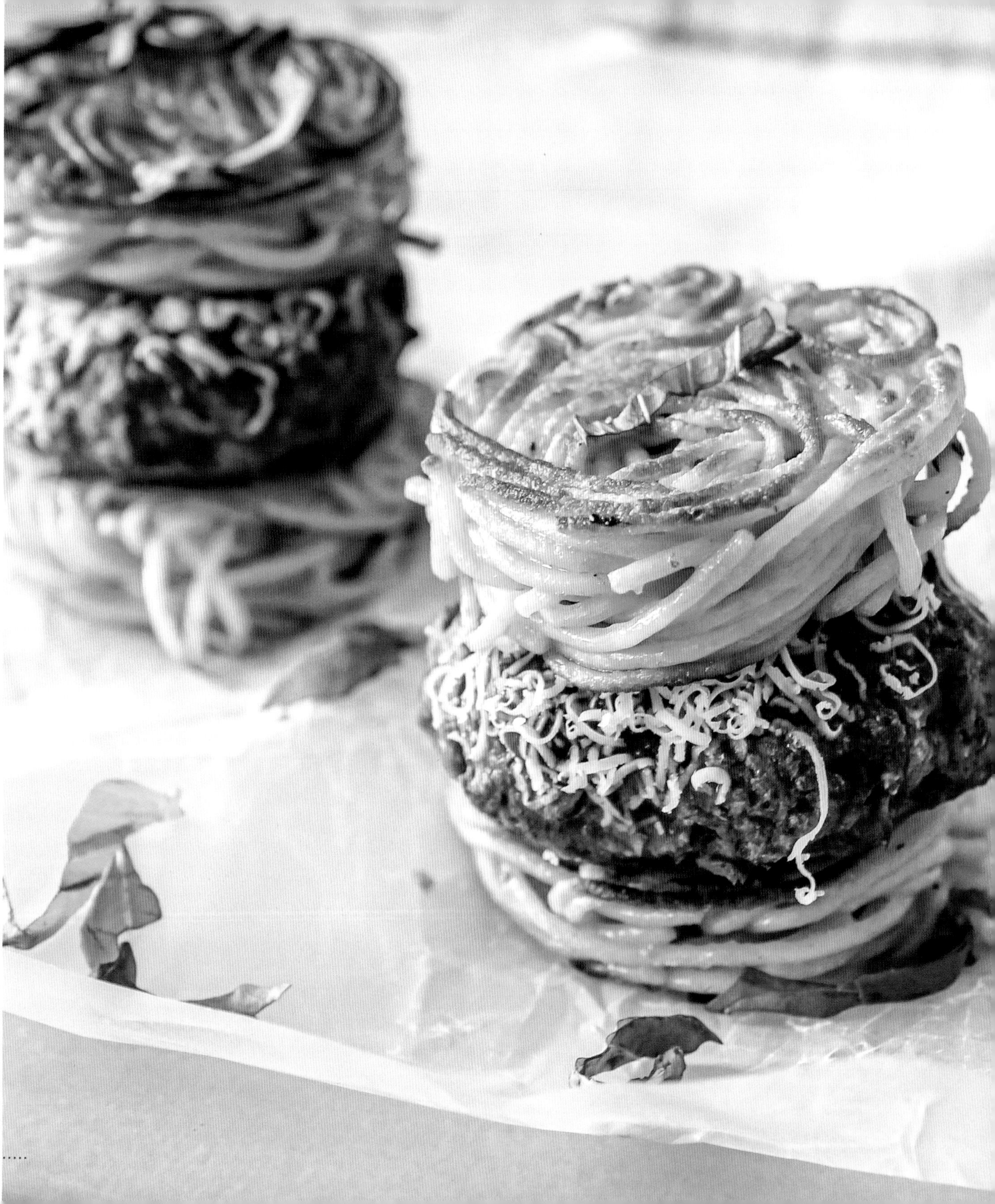

INGREDIENTS:

Fill It Up!

½ cup ricotta cheese

10 basil leaves, chopped

1 handful parsley, chopped

1 teaspoon red pepper flakes

4 tablespoons parmesan cheese, shredded

3 teaspoons oregano

2 pounds ground beef

½ cup bread crumbs

2 teaspoons salt

1 teaspoon black pepper

2 eggs

Half a jar of your favorite marinara sauce

Top It Off!

4 eggs

1 pound spaghetti, cooked and cooled

1 teaspoon garlic powder

1 teaspoon oregano

¾ cup parmesan cheese, shredded, divided

Half a jar of your favorite marinara sauce

10 basil leaves, whole

Spaghetti Bun & Meatballs

This meatball recipe is one of my "dream big" recipes! This was the first recipe I did for ChopHappy.com. Years ago, I was sad about something when Tom and I saw a contest advertised to find the author for Rachael Ray's next cookbook. To cheer me up, Tom entered me in the contest. This was the first recipe I ever truly created on my own. Although I did not win, I made it to the top ten and it was the start of my blog. So these meatballs are now my "dream big," "good luck," and "anything is possible" recipe! I hope you dream big too! I am cheering you on.

INSTRUCTIONS

1. Preheat the oven to 425 degrees.

2. In a large bowl, mix together the ricotta, basil, parsley, red pepper flakes, parmesan, and oregano.

3. Add the beef, bread crumbs, salt, pepper, and 2 eggs. Mix everything together with your non dominant hand; this will avoid overmixing.

4. Form the meat into four patties and place on a parchment paper-lined baking sheet.

5. Bake for 20 minutes before topping each meatball with a few spoonfuls of marinara sauce and baking for an additional 15 minutes. Set aside.

6. Whisk 4 eggs together.

7. Add the whisked eggs to the cooled spaghetti, as well as the garlic powder, oregano, ½ cup of parmesan cheese, and 2 tablespoons of marinara sauce.

8. Place a biscuit cutter in a pan on medium high heat. Pour a teaspoon of vegetable oil into the biscuit cutter. Fill the biscuit cutter with one-eighth of the spaghetti and cook for 2 minutes until crispy. Flip, add more oil, and cook the other side for another 2 minutes. Take out and let cool. Repeat until you have eight spaghetti buns.

9. Add a meatball to a spaghetti bun. Top with marinara sauce, sprinkle with basil and parmesan cheese, and top with another spaghetti bun; enjoy!

"Food is our common ground,
a universal experience."
—James Beard

Everything *Bagel* *Avocado* Shrimp Sandwich

INGREDIENTS:

Fill It Up!

2 pounds shrimp, raw, peeled, deveined

3 tablespoons extra virgin olive oil

1 teaspoon garlic powder

1 teaspoon salt

1 teaspoon pepper

Juice of half a lemon

Top It Off!

4 avocados

Juice of half a lemon

4 tablespoons Greek yogurt

4 teaspoons cilantro, chopped

3 tablespoons everything bagel seasoning

INSTRUCTIONS

1. Preheat the oven to 400 degrees.

2. On a sheet tray, mix together the shrimp, olive oil, garlic powder, salt, and pepper.

3. Once mixed, spread out the shrimp—so it roasts instead of steams—and cook for 10 minutes. *NOTE: No need to turn the shrimp.*

4. Take the shrimp out of the oven and squeeze on the lemon juice. Mix to combine and set aside to cool.

5. Cut each avocado in half lengthwise, remove the pit and skins, and squeeze on the lemon juice to keep the fruit from browning.

6. Into four of the avocado halves, add 1 tablespoon of Greek yogurt. Scoop on some shrimp and add some cilantro before topping with another avocado half.

7. Sprinkle the top of the avocado with everything bagel seasoning, pressing the seeds lightly to stick to the avocado. Enjoy!

Chapter 6: *Condiments*

Making your own condiments is life-changing flavor—wow!
They're like culinary sunshine on your sandwich and are
so easy to make!

Homemade Pantry *Ketchup*

INGREDIENTS

2 cans (6 ounces each)
tomato paste

½ teaspoon garlic powder

½ teaspoon oregano

½ teaspoon salt

½ teaspoon pepper

2 teaspoons apple cider
vinegar

INSTRUCTIONS

1. Mix all the
ingredients
together.

2. Enjoy!

Tom's *Sriracha* Ketchup

INGREDIENTS

½ cup Homemade Pantry
Ketchup (see recipe
above)

1 tablespoon sriracha

Juice of half a lemon

1 teaspoon garlic powder

1 teaspoon honey

INSTRUCTIONS

1. Mix all the
ingredients
together. *NOTE: If
you want a thinner
ketchup, add 2
tablespoons of water.*

2. Enjoy!

Mama Goldstein's *Russian* Dressing

INGREDIENTS

1 cup mayonnaise

½ cup ketchup

1 tablespoon finely chopped pickles

1 tablespoon pickle juice

2 teaspoons horseradish

1 teaspoon Worcestershire sauce

1 tablespoon grated white onion

1 teaspoon pepper

1 teaspoon garlic powder

INSTRUCTIONS

1. Mix everything together. *NOTE: For a smoother consistency, you can blend the ingredients together.*

2. Chill in the refrigerator for at least 30 minutes before serving.

Beet Ketchup

INGREDIENTS

4 large beets, cooked

½ teaspoon garlic powder

2 tablespoons dill

½ teaspoon oregano

½ teaspoon salt

½ teaspoon pepper

2 teaspoons apple cider vinegar

Juice of half a lemon

INSTRUCTIONS

1. Blend all the ingredients together until smooth.

2. Enjoy!

No-Cook BBQ Sauce

INGREDIENTS

½ cup ketchup

½ tablespoon dijon mustard

1 tablespoon dark brown sugar

2 teaspoons apple cider vinegar

1 teaspoon chili seasoning or taco seasoning

1 teaspoon salt

1 teaspoon pepper

INSTRUCTIONS

1. Mix all the ingredients together.

2. Enjoy!

Burger Sauce

INGREDIENTS

½ cup mayonnaise

½ cup ketchup

1 tablespoon pickled jalapeño, chopped

1 teaspoon dijon mustard

INSTRUCTIONS

1. Mix everything together.

2. Enjoy!

Dijon *Honey Mustard*

INGREDIENTS

½ cup dijon mustard

½ cup honey

1 teaspoon apple cider vinegar

½ teaspoon salt

INSTRUCTIONS

1. Mix all the ingredients together.

2. Enjoy!

Arugula *Pesto*

INGREDIENTS

1 clove of garlic

¼ cup shelled pistachios

2 cups arugula

15 basil leaves

1 teaspoon salt

1 teaspoon pepper

1 teaspoon red wine vinegar

½ cup parmesan cheese, shredded

Juice of half a lemon

½ cup extra virgin olive oil

INSTRUCTIONS

1. Place the garlic and pistachios in a blender; pulse to a granular consistency.

2. Add the arugula, basil, salt, pepper, red wine vinegar, parmesan, and lemon juice.

3. Turn the blender on and slowly add the oil; pulse until everything is combined. Enjoy!

Chapter 6: Condiments

Blue Cheese Dressing

INGREDIENTS

¼ cup blue cheese, crumbled

1 large clove of garlic, grated

1 handful parsley, chopped

1 small handful dill, chopped

Zest of 1 lemon

Juice of half a lemon

3 scallions, chopped

1 cup whole-fat Greek yogurt

Big pinch of salt

Big pinch of pepper

INSTRUCTIONS

1. Mix all of the ingredients together in a bowl.

2. Enjoy! *NOTE: For best results, let this dressing marinate between 1 hour and overnight.*

Extra *Creamy Homemade* Mayonnaise

INGREDIENTS

3 egg yolks, room temperature

1 teaspoon dijon mustard

Juice of half a lemon

1¼ cups olive oil

1 teaspoon salt

1 teaspoon pepper

1 teaspoon garlic powder

1 teaspoon apple cider vinegar

INSTRUCTIONS

1. Place the egg yolks, mustard, and lemon juice in a food processor.

2. Turn the food processor on and slowly add the oil.

3. Once the texture is thick and creamy, add the rest of the ingredients and pulse to combine. Enjoy!

Chapter 6: Condiments

About *the Author*

JASON GOLDSTEIN is a chiropractor by day and food blogger by night. Through his culinary blog, *Chop Happy*, Jason shares his love of easy comfort food recipes, showcasing rich flavors, inventive ideas, and unique cooking tips and advice. He was a finalist on *Next Food Network Star* Season 14 and finished in the Top 10 in Rachael Ray's Cookbook Contest. His recipes have been featured on *The Chew* and *The Kitchen*, and he has appeared on *Good Morning America*. Living in NYC and the Hamptons, Jason enjoys testing recipes on his husband, Tom, and grabbing french fries by the handful.

About *Familius*

VISIT OUR WEBSITE: WWW.FAMILIUS.COM

Familius is a global trade publishing company that publishes books and other content to help families be happy. We believe that the family is the fundamental unit of society and that happy families are the foundation of a happy life. We recognize that every family looks different, and we passionately believe in helping all families find greater joy. To that end, we publish books for children and adults that invite families to live the Familius Ten Habits of Happy Family Life: love together, play together, learn together, work together, talk together, heal together, read together, eat together, give together, and laugh together. Founded in 2012, Familius is located in Sanger, California.

CONNECT

Facebook: www.facebook.com/paterfamilius
Twitter: @familiustalk, @paterfamilius1
Pinterest: www.pinterest.com/familius
Instagram: @familiustalk

FAMILIUS

*The most important work you ever do
will be within the walls of your own home.*